268·01

JC

D1374973

New Kid
in the Pew

INTERNATIO.
CHRISTIAN COL

The United
(SCOC)
Library

INTERNATIONAL CHRISTIAN COLLEGE

T043470

Also by Mary Duckert

Help! I'm a Sunday School Teacher

New Kid in the Pew

SHARED MINISTRY WITH CHILDREN

MARY DUCKERT

WESTMINSTER/JOHN KNOX PRESS
Louisville, Kentucky

TISEC

To the teachers and elders at
Woodlands United Reformed Church,
Blackburn, Lancashire, United Kingdom,
who moved over and made room for children

© 1991 Mary Duckert

All rights reserved—no part of this book may be reproduced in any form
without permission in writing from the publisher, except by a reviewer
who wishes to quote brief passages in connection with a review in maga-
zine or newspaper.

The scripture quotation marked RSV is from the Revised Standard Version
of the Bible, copyright 1946, 1952, © 1971, 1973 by the Division of Christian Education of the National Council of the Churches of Christ in the
U.S.A., and is used by permission.

Unless otherwise identified, scripture quotations are from the New Revised Standard Version of the Bible, copyright © 1989 by the Division of
Christian Education of the National Council of the Churches of Christ in
the U.S.A., and are used by permission.

Book design by Publishers' WorkGroup

First Edition

Published by Westminster/John Knox Press
Louisville, Kentucky

PRINTED IN THE UNITED STATES OF AMERICA

9 8 7 6 5 4 3 2 1

Library of Congress Cataloging-in-Publication Data

Duckert, Mary.
   New kid in the pew : shared ministry with children / Mary Duckert.
   — 1st ed.
        p.   cm.
   ISBN 0-664-25206-0

   1. Children—Religious life.   2. Children in church work.
I. Title
BV4571.2.D83 1991
259'.22—dc20   91-17579

Contents

Introduction:
New Kid in the Pew

David Engstrom stood before the congregation. He held three Bibles in his hands. "Will the following people please come forward," he said. "Dan Park, Matthew Campbell, and Fiona Darwin."

Three children looked up at the minister, who was dressed in a white belted robe with a green stole.

"Last year at this time I told the congregation that unless things changed there would be no second graders to receive Bibles in another year," the pastor said. "Danny, Matt, and Fiona, you are gifts from God to this church."

He gave each child a Bible and was about to offer a prayer.

"Then"—as he tells the story now—"I did something I had not planned to do at all. I said to the children, 'We're going to thank God that you came to Covenant Church. If you were the minister, what would you pray?'"

Fiona Darwin answered quickly, eyes focused somewhere over David Engstrom's head. "O God, you dinna ha' to do it. But thanks anyway for me very own Bible. Amen."

The minister offered a prayer of thanks, and the children turned to sit down.

Dan Park had come in November from Korea with his parents and two sisters. Matthew Campbell had just come from an adoption agency to be a son and brother in a family of four. Fiona Darwin and her mother had lived in rural Scotland and Liverpool before moving once again in April. The casual observer would have seen an Asian, an African-American, and a Caucasian.

1

Casual observations and hasty assumptions have seldom been accurate concerning children. But today's churches are filled with lively exceptions to old rules of thumb. Even with trained eyes, we are in for surprises. These children behave differently from those of even one generation ago. Most remarkable to professional church child-watchers is their stalwart insistence on being included. Many of these children are not deeply rooted in a congregation by virtue of family ties to the church. Some of them have a relationship with two congregations as they spend time with divorced parents. Others, victims of adults' thoughtlessness and abuse, have come to find a safe place in a particular congregation. Many are children in one-parent homes who have been taught to look after themselves. They relate to responsible adults in the community and become members of the institutions that offer them recreation, education, and worship. Almost all the church's children are wary of adults until they prove trustworthy on the children's own terms. Children today do not take safety for granted.

It is no wonder that the God of the child Isaac, Moses, Samuel, and Jesus calls these children to worship, learn, and work for others in the church. Nor is it an accident that in congregations where these young members are involved in *shared ministry*, there is no place and no person completely safe from the purposes of God.

WHAT IS SHARED MINISTRY?

The apostles, of necessity, were in a shared ministry. The Christians found early in their new life together that the apostles were too busy preaching and teaching to do all the work of the community. That is why deacons came to be. When churches in Corinth and Philippi were served by itinerant preachers, the ministry was shared again and again. How else could the Word be preached and taught and the sacraments administered?

In our day, shared ministry most often refers to what ministers and adult and teenage members do to carry out the work of the church. In shared ministry, clergy and church educators are employed to discover, encourage, educate, and work alongside laity. Children are most often outside the limits of shared ministry except as the beneficiaries of adult leadership. Because they are not ready to be deacons and elders, what ministry they can do is most often accomplished through the church school. Where church school projects are launched with enthusiasm and completed with visible results, the children benefit. Where children are intentionally included as contributors to and recipients of shared ministry, the program of the whole church is enlivened in worship, education, and work for others.

A clergy couple moved from positions in a multiple-staff church to be co-pastors of two small churches in and near a town of fifteen hundred people. The pastoral search committee was enthusiastic about the couple's commitment to what they called "shared ministry."

"What a surprise!" the woman said as she recounted their experiences at a continuing education seminar. "We thought we knew about shared ministry. But *everyone* in the town church was ministering in some way. It's a way of life. Our six-year-old daughter stays with a member after school a couple of days a week to do 'disciple work' with the woman. They made and delivered a casserole to someone. She drew a picture to go in a letter to a missionary."

"What more can you offer as ministers in such a place?" a young pastor inquired of her.

"Kev and I have talked about that," the woman answered. "The town church has the machinery going, but there's no limit to the depth or extent of the ministry. We haven't made a difference in the injustice right around us. The children work hard, but their participation in worship isn't significant. We have more than enough that we can do. And there's the church in the country—they need us."

Shared ministry is more than busywork for children. At the very least, the efforts should make a difference to the church and to those the church serves. At the very most, all efforts in worship, education, and service are an emphatic response to the Great Commandments of the Old and New Testaments—love God and our neighbors as ourselves. In between, we would do well to strive for intentional memory building, by making an earnest effort to provide vivid experiences in the lives of the gathered people of God which are indeed *worthy* of memory.

INCLUDING CHILDREN IN MINISTRY

There have long been two ways congregations included children as doers and receivers in the work and worship of the church: (1) expecting school age children to do specific jobs as part of a large project, and (2) accepting any age child as a tag-along in places where parents and care givers are at work and worship.

More often than not such inclusion is not considered part of the children's education, but rather something wholesome to do with others in the church. Most of the first variety of all-church projects in which children have responsibility are accomplished through the church school and, as such, are inclusive. The second involvement depends on a child's close relationship to an active adult member in order to gain inclusion. Both kinds of associations with the church can result in events that are memorable and worthy of memory. Those memories affect the attitudes toward the purposes of the church that we bring with us to adulthood.

If we plan now to include children in shared ministry in significant work that they could not possibly do by themselves, we are beginning the practice of intentional memory building. We are enlarging the children's curriculum to include worship, music, and discipleship in the community and beyond. Undergirding all our attempts is a biblical education in the church school. We are expanding the time children spend on church-related activities and bringing the influence of the church into the world. We are increasing the number of young people and adults who are teachers of children as they relate to one another in shared ministry. Instead of a proliferation of unrelated activities for a variety of groups, the end result in program planning is fewer activities with greater impact.

In Bethany Church, a congregation of nearly two hundred in the northeastern United States with a tradition of making homes for refugees, the concept of shared ministry did not become a working principle until the last pastoral change. A middle-aged former city planner and second-career minister was chosen as the new pastor. He was the father of two teenagers and stepfather of nine-year-old twins. He recognized the signs of shared ministry in the refugee resettlement work only. When the officers bemoaned their struggling church school, he discovered that it was confined to children from two years of age to those in sixth grade. After asking many questions, he told them he had a hunch that if they ran the educational enterprise the way they managed refugee hospitality, things would change for the better.

There was immediate interest. The officers discussed some characteristics of the refugee projects.

Preparation of living quarters and furnishings was organized by a couple who found work for everybody. As the time approached for the family to arrive, they posted a large chart in the narthex. It listed responsibilities, names of volunteers, and spaces for still more people to sign up where help was needed. Each major responsibility had one or two persons in charge. Those people had to teach other volunteers if the work demanded special skill or knowledge.

A small committee cooperated with the agency receiving refugees and arranged employment possibilities. Where there were school-age children, a group of adults, young people, and younger boys and girls arranged for ways to welcome them to the community, school, and church. The rule with this group was to work two by two, never alone.

The last point the officers brought up was, "We have always had fun doing it." They told the minister about taking two vans to the airport forty miles away for an 8 P.M. arrival. The children and young people had made welcome signs in Polish. A woman and her eleven-year-old son made up the family they were meeting. Two fifth graders, the official welcomers, and three preschoolers belonging to other volunteers were to hold up the welcome signs. One of the drivers taught everyone Polish words and phrases from a Berlitz book. Then he engaged the entire group in a game, using what they had learned. When a fifth grader won, the leader said it was because the boy had a "young brain." The plane, when it arrived, was three hours late and did not carry the family's baggage. The children had all fallen asleep.

Both intentional and casual inclusion of children was part of the experience. All the participants benefited from the game leader's sense of fun. No one was expected to do something without help. When the children became tired it was all right to sleep. The adults relating the story remembered the usual annoyances of late planes and missing luggage with much laughter. The minister had good reason to hope for more of that spirit loosed in the church.

In the minister's second year in the congregation there was an all-church retreat. The program committee staged a town meeting at which recognition was given for work well done and the contents of a Best Things at Bethany box were read and discussed. (The officers had requested suggestions of memorable times and events that might be worth repeating.)

The five older children in the church school had taken the assignment seriously and submitted sealed envelopes with their suggestions in them. Their teacher planned for the class to poll the younger children and include their "best things" all on one sheet of paper.

In reflecting on the responses, the minister said two features were prominent: (1) The adults prized well-attended events, and (2) the children remembered doing things they had done for the first time. The younger children's opinion poll yielded singing in church, planting tulip bulbs, cleaning out the supplies closet, going to Mrs. Carlsen's house to sing for her, and, to the minister's delight, learning to read from the Bible.

What Motivates the Pastor?

Bethany Church's minister has his own professional goals for the congregation. They are on their way but not near achievement.

"The church school," he reports, "is not large but it is growing. What it lacks in numbers it makes up for in vitality. It helps to have four kids of our own to put into it. There hadn't been a class of adolescents for thirty years. Bible study for all church school teachers and leaders is a reality. I lead it.

"But," he continues, "my goal is to make Bible study the core of all activity that goes on in the name of shared ministry. Only the teachers, children, and teenagers have the privilege of hands-on Bible study right now.

"It was through Bible study that God called me to go to seminary. It wasn't community organization and city planning projects. They didn't have the dynamism by themselves. For two years in a row I attended a three-day lay academy led by a professor of philosophy. He opened the scriptures to me. He talked in simpler language than our fifth-grade twins. Each year, it was a different study, but he kept coming back to the same questions: What did this mean to the people who heard it? What differences does it make to us? My work at City Hall took on a new meaning, but I came to realize I had to do some more Bible study and also to teach others."

Shared Worship and Education

Children's presence in corporate worship is no longer rare. The children themselves feel they belong there, especially when they have a contribution to make. Not all adult members and not all pastors are at ease with children present. A good bit has been written to encourage doubters in both Roman Catholic and Protestant churches. Some denominations have gone on record or amended their constitutions to invite children to the Lord's Supper.

The coolness adult members display toward sharing the place of worship with children stems generally from unexplained changes in the order of worship. They are especially cool to action songs and litanies using contemporary slang. A pastor's reservations may be rooted in his or her lack of skill in talking with a group of children. Deportment of the children is rarely the reason adults fail to appreciate their presence. Parents of young children sometimes prefer to worship without being concerned about what their offspring do.

There are fairly uncomplicated resolutions to these feelings, which benefit the whole community of worshipers. They are spelled out in chapter 5.

In many congregations the presence of children is an accepted tradition. The issue in those congregations is one of finding appropriate expressions of worship for all the people gathered. We are not *sharing* worship if the words and actions are out of reach of the comprehension of children. Neither are we serving God and our neighbors if we provide entertainment for children more suitable at a picnic than in a house of prayer.

A woman who has been in rural and small-town ministry for over twenty years discovered shared worship in her present position in the Midwest. The Sunday she was called to the pastorate she noted that the children sat together in the front of the sanctuary for about ten minutes and then left.

At the picnic after the congregational meeting she asked some of the children, "Where did you go this morning during the service of worship? Why didn't you stay?"

The children were forthright in replying. They went to the basement. They left because they always had.

"I would like to have you stay if you want," she said.

"We'll have to ask our teacher," a girl of seven told the new minister.

That small conversation, with no condescension on the part of the woman or any trepidation felt by the children, began a relationship with integrity and purpose.

The school-age children began spending time in their enrichment class learning to use the hymnal, to follow the order of service, and to find and read the scripture selections. They spent every other Sunday for three months learning the skills necessary for informed worship in that congregation. On alternate Sundays they attended services.

The minister is an experienced storyteller. She used the art form in different ways in her sermon composition. While the schoolchildren were learning to listen to sermons, her texts included the parable of the Prodigal Son and Peter's denial of Jesus. At the beginning of each sermon she told the Bible story. On Pentecost Sunday she told the stories of the confusion of tongues at the tower of Babel and of the understanding that came when God sent the Holy Spirit in Jerusalem. After the Pentecost service she and a sixth-grade girl were talking. "I love your stories, Mrs. Thiesen," she said. "They all end the same way, don't they? God says, 'OK, shape up. I'll give you one more chance!'"

The pastor is in her fourth year at the church. Older children — not adults — teach the younger ones how to use the tools of worship and how to listen to sermons.

In shared ministry, children can learn to do the work of disciples, evangelists, and next-door neighbors. As they become students of the Bible, they are eager to respond to scripture in their work in the world and in their worship. Education, work for and with the neighbor, and worship of God are the ingredients of the church experience of all of us in shared ministry.

"What shall we do?" the people asked after Peter's sermon on the Day of Pentecost.

That is what this book is about.

1

A Place for Children

Children who have spent Sunday morning at church for five or six years of their lives know where they belong and where they don't. They teach other children eventually by example and terse instructions.

A preschool child had often accompanied her grandmother to a weekly gathering of quilters in the basement of their church. She used to stand on a chair in front of a movable chalkboard drawing with chalk and erasing until the quilters called, "Party time, Sweetie!" On Sundays she found out very quickly that standing on chairs was forbidden, only adults used the movable chalkboard, and no one called her "Sweetie."

When she was five a new young neighbor accompanied her and her family to church school. "Now I will teach you what to do," she told her new friend on the ride to the church. "You must behave or there will be trouble." But no information followed her forecast of doom.

Her father said, "I'm waiting, Katie. What are you going to tell Alison to do?"

"I am not going to *tell* her anything, Daddy," the child answered. "She has to watch me. All grown-ups at church can tell all kids what to do. And we never know what that will be."

There was a gulf between the official planners' understanding of *space* for boys and girls and Katie's grasp of *place* in the church building and in the congregation.

WHERE DO CHILDREN BELONG?

Within the last thirty years there has been increasing interest in the early exposure of children to the whole program of the church. They are encouraged to attend worship and all-church mission festivals. They go on walks for hunger relief and have been seen peeping out of canvas baby bags at protest marches.

During the same period we have experienced changes in the nature of teaching and the attitude toward classroom space for children. As more and more women work outside the home, the whole family has less time for volunteer work—for preparation of teaching sessions, for teacher education classes, workshops, and week-long summer schools.

In many congregations children do not see the same teacher week after week during the church school year. Their class area may not reflect the content of the teaching and learning. It takes time and energy to plan for an adequate place for children. But it is the responsibility of the church to do it, one way or another.

The room or class area should say to the children, This is your place in the church. It is your launching pad and your splash-down area. It is where you are counted when you come and where you are missed when you don't.

A man and a woman volunteered to teach eight second and third graders in a well-attended old downtown church in northern New England. Their teacher's guide suggested that the children draw self-portraits as a means of getting acquainted.

"We fantasized about how we could redecorate the room," the woman said. "It took six weeks and a lot of encouragement to get eight portraits. Two boys and a girl are from homes of separated parents. One of the boys goes to two churches. The others don't go anywhere when they visit their fathers."

The man laughed at his and his spouse's persistence. "I called them. Ellen called them. The kids sent hand-made cards pleading with them to come. Our minister suggested we go over with a bullhorn to the homes of the last holdouts and shout, 'We know you're in there. Come out and come to church!'"

The morale in the class is high. The couple believes that the efforts of everyone to get all eight portraits on the walls prodded the boys and girls into caring about one another. During Christmas vacation the teachers mentioned having a party. The children were delighted, but finding the right date was of major importance, because all eight had to be there, they said. The teachers were intending to have the party in their home. "Why can't we have it in our room?" a child asked. They did.

With the security of having a place to return to in the church, even very young children can find themselves at ease in other places on the church grounds. They may prepare snacks for an open house, using the kitchen. They may contribute to an art show in a corridor, take a new song to another class and teach others to sing it, or put a letter to a homebound person in a nearby mailbox.

Older children develop a proprietary feeling toward their space at church. They like to leave their mark, and initials on tables or graffiti on walls may not be appreciated. They are eager to move on to claim another space but develop a nostalgia for places that belonged to them at one time.

A small church in the upper Midwest meets in the basement for all church school classes while another denomination has worship upstairs. The adults are in the kitchen. The infants, toddlers, and two-year-olds are in a room with cribs, a rocking chair, and toys. The three-, four-, and five-year-olds are on a platform. All other classes are in the dining room. When children enter the early elementary class, they have a group snapshot made and framed for the dining room wall. When boys and girls finish confirmation class they have another group picture taken and framed for the wall. Before anyone moves away, someone takes a picture for a bulletin board in the back of the dining room.

It is the custom in the congregation to have receptions in the dining room after weddings and memorial services. The pictures are conversation pieces for young and old together. In that congregation, children belong *to* the church and *in* the church.

WHAT KINDS OF SPACE FOR CHILDREN?

At the "rededication," as the congregation called it, of their redeveloped church in a postindustrial city in the Northeast, the architect spoke.

"I am a Baptist deacon, and you are Presbyterians and Episcopalians. But on this point we agree: This is a house of prayer and a place of ministry. Do you wonder why the largest spaces in this church are for the worship of God and the education of young children? Do you question a fifty-thousand-dollar ramp leading from the parking lot to those two spaces? If a church is to be a house of prayer to all people, it has to be accessible. If it is to be a place for ministry to all people, they need access to where that ministry happens. The ministry that children of two, three, and four years of age perform in the interest of all of us is best carried out in rooms where they can live and move in a neighborly way. They take up more space than those of us who have learned to read, write, and think sitting on folding chairs. Every person in this congregation was included in the architectural plan. This is my ministry."

There were three people in wheelchairs at the service. One was five years old. Two were in their eighties. The minister said he had met all three on the street, invited them for test runs, and told them not to miss the rededication.

The architect understood that children engage in ministry as they learn in the church. Many adult Christians think of children as recipients of ministry, and so they are. We are all recipients of ministry. The privilege of ministering unto others is given to children only where parents, teachers, church officers, and ministers want it to happen. They need space to do it.

Older Elementary Ministry

Boys and girls of eight to twelve years of age want permission to enter the world of concerns that young people and adults appear to share in the church. They are stalwart supporters of the underdog and the disenfranchised. They want to feed the hungry and make peace where there is none, but they don't know how. More than any other group, they need the security of consistent adult leadership in their launching pad and splash-down area. Their class area may be tables and chairs, chalkboard, and a supplies cupboard with Bibles, reference books, and art materials.

The church, community, and world make up their learning environment. They may be in a choir that sings occasionally at corporate worship. They may be involved in community ministry or justice issues through school or scouts. We want them to bring all they are and do to their space at church. They want to make a difference in the world, and the church is the place equipped to help them.

All teachers, leaders, tutors, and coaches of older children need to give the same instructions about use of the building and procedures concerning trips away from the building. The children can be expected to remember one set of such instructions, but not a different set from every adult who serves them as an adviser.

Some church officers issue instructions relating to safe, sane, and sanitary uses of the building. Some Christian education committees determine rules for field trips and outdoor adventure.

A southern California suburban church board of elders

requested that fourth and fifth graders submit their own rules. The junior highs had already done so. The intention was that, by establishing the rules, the children would remember them and want to obey them. A teacher, scout leader, and choir director met with the children on a Sunday morning. Some rules came quickly and made sense to everyone. Some were disputed, such as "Don't play the piano if you don't know how" and "The last person out of the building turns out the lights."

It became evident that children of ten, eleven, and twelve years of age do not have the experience, wisdom, and judgment to suggest appropriate rules for their space at church and their behavior elsewhere.

A fifth-grade girl asked, "Who wants us to do this, Mr. Lund?"

"The elders have asked us leaders to work with you, Janna," the man answered.

"I think," Janna said, "that we need to make an agreement or something. You know, like a contract. The elders promise and the kids promise and the teachers promise." The children agreed with her suggestion. Two elders volunteered to work with a committee of adult advisers, young people, and older children to draw up a covenant. They worked one hour each Sunday for a month before they had a first draft to take back to the children, young people, and adult leadership, including the elders. With remarkably few objections and additions, the covenant was accepted.

There is a copy of it hanging in every gathering place in the church. It was published in the church newsletter; drivers, adult assistants, and invited guests receive copies before they go on excursions away from the church. The minister assumes that there will be a need at least every autumn for a renewal of the covenant. "It does no good if we forget about it. The Bible is full of stories to back me up on that," he told the congregation in a sermon.

Such a covenant informs the congregation of the nature

of the older children's educational experience. Two or three children need to do research and conduct an interview to learn about memorial gifts. Two children choose to tape-record an opinion poll on the treatment of homeless families. One's mental picture of Sunday school for a class of eleven-year-olds may change. The boys and girls are not just sitting around a table staring at a teacher. That image is still valid, but it is not the only one.

When children are enlisted to accompany adults on home visits during stewardship drives, they are there learning to be responsible members and eventual officers of a congregation. They receive training before they go, although not the same instruction as the adults.

A small church at the edge of a college community in the Northwest incorporated older children in the total program of the church throughout the tenure of one pastor. College students and children did what they called "acts of mercy" for the neighborhood's elderly. The children received orientation from a deacon who taught psychology at the college. She and the college students involved the children in role-playing situations with debriefing. Their emphasis was on being neighbors and serving neighbors. In the role play the college student took the lead but would involve the child in conversation with the neighbor and encourage the child to help in appropriate ways.

After an actual visit, the students were expected to talk over the experience with the children. The work varied. They took walks to the prescription pharmacy, read aloud to those with limited sight, delivered groceries, visited and listened to lengthy stories about long ago. More than once a visiting team alerted the pastor in time to correct or prevent a problem noticed during the visit.

Younger Children's Ministry

Kindergarten and first-grade children are enthusiastic about what they call "disciple work." It is done two by two, at least, and never alone. It is based on the story in Luke 10 of Jesus sending out the seventy to bring healing and peace. Although in many congregations the work involves small projects for others within the church, there are some delightful exceptions. The work is best begun with a few children and a helper in a homelike, spacious area in the church. To reinforce the concept of disciple work, devote an entire session once a month for at least three months. Set up three or four projects in the children's own space.

One of the reasons disciple work needs room is that all projects are cooperative; all children learn to choose the work they prefer to do with an adult or young person. All work is just hard enough so that no child can finish it alone but can complete it with satisfaction with the help of someone older.

All children meet with their helpers and teachers to begin with. They divide the work and go to smaller work areas to complete it. When they are finished, they return to the gathering place to hear reports and look at some of the work. Some projects require that small groups contribute to one large job. Coming together, then, is essential to completing the project.

Here are some examples of younger children's disciple work, all of which can be completed in one session of church school. Some have been done in borrowed space, arranged ahead of time by adults. Some were carried out in the children's own class area. The important issue is that five-, six-, and seven-year-olds have work to do in the church and need space in which to do it.

1. Births, Baptisms, and Adoptions. A one-Sunday activity was so deeply appreciated by parents, grandparents, officers, and pastor that young children have made it their ongoing disciple work. It is their job to welcome newborns and newly adopted children by sending them letters. Sometimes it is the first letter a child receives. The letters are original, with more illustration than printed sentiments. The first ones to newborns said *Welcome to the world* and had colorful flowers pasted around the message. In two years both the teachers and the children became more innovative. A recent letter written on shelf paper began, *You're going to like it here. These are the things we like.* There were drawings and pictures cut from magazines of people, animals, roses, pizza, spacecraft; as the minister noted, "Kermit the Frog was the only reference to TV."

Newly adopted children are a great curiosity, especially to other adopted children in the class. The teachers find out what they can about the child and family. There have been three adoptions in two years. The most recent addition to the church family was a four-year-old sister to a child in the class. The children decided to make a little book introducing her to her new family, new church, and new town. The teacher said it would take too long for them to do such a book.

"I will ask my father to help us. He's an artist," one child said. With permission and a note, he and his friend went to the adult class and came back with a man who makes a living drawing cartoons. The children designed the book and dictated the words, and together the artist and the children decided what to illustrate.

At every baptism this class presents an original welcome card or letter. Some of the baptized are adults who are also joining the church. The children are present for the baptisms, and one child is appointed to give the missive to the parent or baptized person.

2. For Young Children Who Wait. A Roman Catholic sister told her family that what she needed most in her work with displaced Hispanic families in Chicago was kits for children who have to wait.

"They wait for their parents. They wait to see a nurse. They wait at the bus station. They spend hours waiting, with nothing to do," she complained. Her parents told the neighbors, and soon a community project was afoot. The sister requested denim envelopes with a small box of crayons and paper. The kindergarten children at a community vacation church school assembled the kits — over a hundred of them. As they worked, one of the girls asked her teacher, "Would you mind if I drew a heart and wrote my name in one of these?" The teacher seized the opportunity to form a bond between givers and receivers. She gave small index cards to the other teachers and passed on the child's question. All the kits arrived in Chicago with love notes.

3. The Library That Grows. A woman in India writing to a friend in Hawaii said, "You always ask what you can do. Now I finally have something for you. We need picture books for our nursery." The friend told the Christian education coordinator in her church, who wrote an item in the newsletter asking for books the children had outgrown. Because the church serves a military installation, the coordinator included the name and address of the woman in India.

The young children were instantly interested in gathering and sending books. They packed a dozen at a time, choosing one to read aloud before putting all of them in a box or large envelope. The woman who had received the request took the older children to the library to look for books about India. They read and showed them to the young children who were giving away their picture books.

Months after they sent the first books, a letter came from India. It said, *Thank you, friends from Oahu. We like our new library.* It was signed with thumbprints of the children in the nursery. By the time the letter got to the church, some families had already moved on to other military installations, and new children in the church brought books. The woman in India began getting packages from Alabama, California, Pennsylvania, and Mannheim, Germany.

Young children need the help of adults to carry out such a ministry, but it need not be confined to their own congregation, community, or country.

4. "We Are Thinking of You" Cards. A former day-school teacher in a retirement community in Arizona began a church school class for visiting children. Some days there is no one for her to teach, and she goes to her own study group. One of the activities she always includes is the making of cards that say, *We are thinking of you.* She explains to the children that grandparents and great-grandparents often need "cheer-up" cards. She collects the cards in a photo album with double acetate pages so that they stay clean and unwrinkled. Each church school session the children hear a story about someone in the community who needs a card. They choose one, sign it, and send it before they make new ones for the album.

The woman's neighbors continue to appreciate the children's cards. As the young artists return on visits they seek out their teacher, who has now appropriated a "children's place" in the large meeting room with a small table and four chairs, books to read, and basic art materials for those who prefer to cut, color, draw, paint, and paste.

Youngest Children's Ministry

The ministry that the youngest children perform in the church is largely to one another. The space for two-, three-, and four-year-olds needs to be homelike, clean, and safe. Boys and girls who have been on earth twenty-four to forty-eight months may have had a variety of day-care experiences or a more limited nursery school exposure. Most are still learning how to cope with other children in an unfamiliar environment.

The church experience remains unfamiliar to these young children for some time. For them the week between Sundays is more like a month. There may be strange faces each time they come, even if one adult remains constant. Those children who come infrequently may not be recognized by anyone upon repeat visits.

The space for these boys and girls should allow for individual activities, small-group activities, and some limited interaction with the whole group.

Denominationally prepared curriculum materials offer ways for adults to welcome the nestlings, accustom them to their surroundings, and ultimately help them become responsible for some of the order, cleanliness, and safety of their environment. As the year progresses, the prepared curriculum materials offer ways for regularly attending children to welcome newcomers and make them feel comfortable.

The rate of growth and maturation in this age range is astounding. The changes, for good or ill, are dramatic. Most early childhood workers with enough experience to generalize with accuracy prefer that two-year-olds have separate accommodations from three-and four-year-olds. The reason is that their behavior, as they grow from toddlers to preschoolers, is erratic and highly individualistic. Three-year-olds, on the other hand, are learning many new social skills. When they are with four-year-olds they imitate those skills. Unfortunately, when they are with two-year-olds there is a tendency to regress.

Two-year-olds do well by themselves with a good bit of space and worthwhile equipment. If there are one, two, or three on the class roll they are better served to be viewed as big brothers and sisters of crawlers and toddlers than to be negative models for the older preschoolers.

Curriculum materials for these age groups give guidance on relevant and appropriate equipment and room arrangements.

Frequent attenders of this age range tend to take possession of their allotted space. Some children are almost pastoral in their care of a newcomer or someone who has been absent. In some churches two-year-olds are promoted to the next class during the year somewhere near their third birthday. It is best to have two fledglings "fly up" at the same time. They might be taken for a visit as children are arriving, introduced to some of the three-year-olds, and given a part in a small-group activity. When the children go to stay they might take something as a gift — flowers, raisins, or a favorite book. If only one child progresses from the two-year-old group, it is wise to visit him or her in the early moments of the session once or twice just to keep in touch.

All preschoolers fare better in their relationships with others at church if they have had frequent and consistent contact with the church outside of their own space. Two-year-olds with able supervision can learn about the church by making a short visit to another group or to an individual worker at every session. It is a worthwhile change-of-pace activity. They become acquainted with the business of the church. Older children, young people, and adults become acquainted with them. They learn that they have a place, others have a place, and they can visit back and forth. Such a visit each week should never assure teachers or parents that two-year-olds left on their own or separated from their group will know the church as they know their own home. They can easily be disoriented in remarkably small buildings. But cordial relationships built up Sunday after Sunday will help a child to trust a teacher in another class, or a designated older child, to take him or her back to the nest.

Newcomers in the older preschool classes may be introduced to the educational work of the church as their seasoned classmates accompany them on a tour of the building. As the veterans explain and interpret, teachers discover misunderstandings and half-truths that may need immediate repair.

On a tour of a large church building just acquired by another denomination, two teachers and five four-year-olds were introducing a young guest to their church. They opened door upon door, peeked in on adult classes, kitchen, storeroom, offices, and a high-ceilinged sanctuary with stained glass windows on three sides.

"Whoa!" one of the teachers exclaimed. "We can look around. There's no one here right now. Let's tell Martin about this room. It belongs to all of us. Who can tell him what happens here?"

"This," said a girl with confidence, "is where people go when they die." She went on to describe a funeral for three children in one family who had died in an apartment fire.

Relating the conversation at a leadership event, the teacher said that by the time the girl had told her story, one of the teachers had the presence of mind to ask her, "Do you know why those people came here that day, Mia?" The child wasn't sure.

The teacher said, "Well, I think I know. This is where we can all come to sing and pray to God." She went to the baptismal font. "Look here," she said. "What's this?"

The children had seen a baptism on Dedication Sunday. They told about it.

The teacher continued. "Grown-ups carried the baby we saw baptized. That's the only way a tiny child of God can get to the church. And at the funeral you told us about, Mia, grown-ups carried those little children out after everybody prayed and sang to God."

Hearing the teachers' story, the leaders asked several questions neither teacher could answer: How did you know what to say? What did the children think? Will the conversation bother them? One question they answered well: What did you do after that?

They all sat down on the chancel steps, the teachers reported. They sang:

"If anybody asks you who I am,
 Say I'm a child of God."

Then they went back to their room.

The sanctuary and other common rooms do indeed belong to everyone. Teacher-conducted tours help define for young children the functions of the rooms, appropriate behavior in them, and the privileges of belonging there.

A Word About Infants in the Church

Many babies and toddlers these days experience day care outside their homes. Some do not. For all infants the church is a strange place to be. It is a new world. The space for their care should be of an even temperature, clean, and safe. Furniture, bedding, and playthings should also be kept clean and safe. Toddlers and creepers need a clean rug on which to sit, crawl, and tumble.

Some of the most welcome features of an otherwise well-equipped room for babies are: (1) windows looking outside or into a corridor alive with purposeful activity, (2) mirrors, (3) a full-size rocking chair, and (4) a cassette recorder with tapes of organ music, choir anthems, and congregational singing. The babies will hear that music again when, as sure-footed, articulate, curious preschoolers, they are part of the worshiping congregation.

This is the first place some children come in a church. They may or may not remain in it long enough to have lasting memories. No matter how mobile the population of Christendom becomes, it is essential that there be in every congregation adequate space and capable care for the newest arrivals on earth, who of necessity are separated from their primary caregivers.

GROUPING AND GRADING

Many congregations have made a tradition of their system of grouping children. If the church has not changed since the tradition began, the system may serve it well. In a rapidly or constantly changing community, the system may well be examined as to its usefulness every spring in anticipation of another curriculum year beginning in September.

Denominational curriculum materials often present one recommended grouping, with alternative suggestions for a more broadly graded class. Many variations are satisfactory. For example, a church school with 150 or more children attending on Sunday in a residential section of a large city has an enrollment of over 300. Just less than half the children attend twice a month. For many years the children were in closely graded classes. Three years ago they were put in two-year groupings. Last year they tried to divide according to attendance. Here is their carefully honed system, which they intend to alter each year based on attendance. Posters inside the front and rear doors give directions to the classes.

> Babies (20 months)
> Almost two and twos
> Threes and fours
> All kindergartners and first-grade choir members
> First and second graders
> Third and fourth graders
> Fourth- and fifth-grade choir members

Based on enrollment and attendance from last year, most second and third graders are neither numerous nor dependable in attendance. They are paired with some first and fourth graders so that classes will have about the same number in them each week. Children in choirs have an integrated curriculum plan, particularly related to worship education and biblical references in the music they are learning.

A small church in a village gathers first- through sixth-grade children in one place and divides the group of about fifteen children between two teachers. First graders and sixth graders know who their teachers are; those in between are never sure which of the two they will have. All children return near the end of the session for singing and a prayer. Their study materials are based on the same biblical content. They sing songs from each age group's materials.

A growing suburban church in the Southeast struggled for several years with the grouping of first and second graders. The curriculum resources the church selected had such a grouping. The difficulty arose from mixing children who could read with those who could not. One year kindergarten and first graders were paired with two teachers.

"It was a congenial class," the director of Christian education commented. "But the issue of reading ability bothered the teachers. Last year the first and second graders were together with the same complaint. Now"—she sighed—"would you believe we have enough first graders for a class of their own, and I still get the same complaint?"

The experience in this church might inform others that grouping will not solve all instructional problems. Teaching techniques with young schoolchildren might well vary enough within any session to allow readers to read and nonreaders to listen, readers to do "word work" and nonreaders to do art or drama work. There are probably more and better reasons to keep readers and nonreaders together in the church than there are to isolate nonreaders from their age group. Congeniality is a sound basis for grouping children for learning in the church, especially if they are able to welcome others into their charmed circle.

In contrast to a group of children who look forward to being together for learning, there are from time to time classes of children who weary teachers as they progress through the church educational system. They are incapable of pleasing themselves as teenagers when their advisers work with them in planning their own programs.

It is a tribute to the faithfulness of those congregations that there is room for malcontents, disturbers of the peace, and whole classes who do not seem to find peace year after year in their association with the church. There are pastors, active elders, and denominational leaders who admit with gratitude that they also had teachers and pastors who refused to give up on them.

A church executive who works in the area of social justice remembers being removed from both his class and corporate worship on the same morning.

"I was ten years old," he recalls. "The pastor came to see me that afternoon. Not my parents. Me. He asked me what bugged me about the church. I couldn't tell him.

"He said, 'Think about it, Joe. Call me when you decide what you don't like about us, and maybe we can fix it with your help.'

"I'm grateful to that man," the executive says. "He started me on my life's work—asking what's wrong and finding folks to help fix it."

IS IT WORTH IT?

Sharing the church's space so that children may join in a vital ministry depends on the decision makers' understanding of the children's *membership* in the church.

In a congregation of nearly three thousand adults and young people, about two hundred children are in attendance each Sunday, in rather cramped quarters. There are five large common rooms where they are not permitted to have classes or even to enter except in the company of an adult. Why? Because there are good carpets on the floor, finely upholstered furniture, and lamps that might break.

A new elder at his first meeting questioned the use of space for children and was told, "The common rooms were decorated with money from faithful old members. We can't insult them by having kids pouring juice on the rugs and scratching the tables. Kids don't pay their way."

The inquirer said, "I came to this church forty years ago wrapped in a blanket. When I was three I was in what we call

Miller Hall. When I was four and five I was in this room. There were no leather-covered chairs, but there was a dandy carpet to sit on. And as a fifth grader I moved into Great Hall. The rug looked pretty much the way it does now. I was proud to bring my cousins to my classes. When Jessie and the boys and I moved back here to live, the first place we visited was this church. I showed them every room, from the sanctuary to the furnace room. And there wasn't one place I ever remember feeling I wasn't welcome as a child. Now, *those* were the days of common rooms!"

The new elder had grown up in the church as a member of the church family. The congregation intentionally and unintentionally nurtured his membership so that he was eager to share the place with others. It is too soon to tell how eager his children will be to do the same thing.

The Christian church reaches out to children, because Jesus once said to his disciples, those closest to him, who should have known better than to exclude boys and girls, "Let the little children come to me, and do not stop them; for it is to such as these that the kingdom of heaven belongs" (Matt. 19:14). The school of the church is not established on the same basis as pay-as-you-see TV. It is not taken away from those boys and girls who cannot pay their way or whose parents or guardians cannot or will not. The school is in the church of Jesus Christ. The space and all the people in it belong to him.

SUMMARY

Children's classrooms are their launching pads and splash-down areas in the church, where they are counted when they come and are missed when they don't.

Older elementary children need a place to meet and study together in the church. Their work with people extends into the whole congregation, community, and world.

Younger boys and girls need room enough for adults and

children to work together on a choice of disciple work, short-term projects done in the interests of others.

Youngest children minister largely to one another. Their space needs to be homelike, clean, and safe, with equipment that encourages individual and small-group activities. Regular tours of the church building help introduce youngest children to people of all ages at work in the church.

Decisions about grouping and grading need to be made each year in relation to enrollment, attendance, and appropriate space available.

2

Learning from the Book of the Church

Children, young people, and adults in a church near Washington, D.C., have as teachers men and women called Belongers. They have completed a year of Bible study and are now teaching and continuing their study. They use denominational curriculum resources with the security that comes from a thorough grounding in the scriptures.

David Innes, teacher of sixth graders, is a man who does some international traveling. On the first Sunday with his new class he introduced a day school administrator a few of the children recognized.

"We are all people of the Book in this church," he said. "Without reading the Bible I don't know how we'd find out we belong to God. Ms. Hiruka and I are in a Bible study class where we're learning enough to start teaching you."

The man's daughter spoke out. "Ms. Hiruka's already a teacher, Daddy."

The woman laughed. "I learned to teach science and to help run your school, Amanda. People of the Book keep studying the scriptures in order to teach others. When your father is working overseas I'll be your teacher. We want all the people of the Book to be learning from it."

One Sunday in January the children gathered with Ms. Hiruka to interview Rabbi Goldberg at a newly established Conservative synagogue. They had their questions written out and a cassette recorder with them. The rabbi was eighty-three years old, he told the class voluntarily. He worked at the synagogue a few hours a week.

"The synagogue is nothing much to look at, but it doesn't need to be," he told the boys and girls. "Do you know why? I'll tell you. We are people of the Book. Come. I'll show you." He showed them the Torah, and he read from Deuteronomy 6:4 in Hebrew. Then he intoned in English, "Hear, O Israel: The LORD is our God, the LORD alone." The boys and girls were enchanted.

They all sat down at a table to record the interview. Ms. Hiruka introduced Bruce, who was to ask the questions. He began, "Will you please tell us about your Hebrew school? What do the children learn?"

"We have Hebrew school so that we have a synagogue," Rabbi Goldberg said. "The children learn the Law. They learn the words of the Torah. We are the people of the Book!" he cried out, raising his arms above his head.

"So are we," Bruce told him. The rabbi rocked back in his chair, smiling.

"So you are indeed," the old man said. Then he leaned forward and fixed his eyes on one child after another. "If every boy and girl in this synagogue could answer as Master Bruce did just now, I would give thanks to our God and say, 'This is enough for me, Lord.'"

When Ms. Hiruka and Mr. Innes met upon his return, she played the tape. "We've taught them something, David!" she exclaimed.

"I believe we have," he answered. "Do you think they're ready now to teach others?"

GETTING TO KNOW THE BIBLE

Forty years ago James Smart, a Canadian pastor and author, wrote, "The church must teach or die." The church's textbook is the Bible. If we in the church do not read it and teach others from it, no one else will. The scriptures of the

Old and New Testaments are blood and muscle to the Body of Christ.

Dr. Smart wrote his warning to adults in the church whose lifelong vocation it is to study the scriptures and teach them by word and deed to others.

But in the schools of the church today there are more children and young people getting to know the Bible than adults pursuing their studies. In the sanctuaries of the congregations on any Sunday morning there are adults at worship who are less familiar with the Old and New Testaments than faithfully attending nine- and ten-year-olds. Fortunately, one effective way to refresh one's memory about the content of the scriptures is to teach children, using responsibly designed and written curriculum resources that are rooted in the scriptures.

THE TEACHER AND THE BIBLE

At a leadership school a free-lance writer reported on her introduction to teaching and to the scriptures.

"'But I don't know zip about the Bible,' I told my pastor when he asked me to teach. 'Every Sunday in church it's all news to me. I don't know what I was doing back there in Sunday school as a kid—nothing stuck.'

"He was patient and persistent. He told me that the Bible isn't like *The Cat in the Hat* or *Charlotte's Web*. It's more like a saga about a family over centuries of time. He said that he got hooked on it in Vietnam. His chaplain was a storyteller who was on very good terms with God. He told the troops that they were the family of God in A.D. 1970, and it was time they read their family album.

"I'm interested in how books get written, who reads them, and why some are bestsellers. I told the pastor I would sit down and read the Bible and then tell him if I would teach. I think he laughed or snorted or tried to do neither.

"'In my experience,' he drawled, 'Bible study with others

is a more effective way of becoming acquainted with the scriptures. Reading the Bible straight through is like trying to read a whole library.'

"About half a dozen of us had a Sunday morning class with him for a couple of months. He assigned us the reading of Genesis, Exodus, John 1, and all of Matthew *before we came.* I got all wrapped up in the Jacob and Joseph story. The next week I read the first twenty chapters of Exodus to my fifteen-year-old daughter. She said it was better than a mini-series on TV.

"When we got to class he gave us an outline of the course he was going to teach. The first two questions I remember clearly: Who is God? What are we created to be and do? During the first session I realized I had been reading without knowing those questions were important at all. By the time the course was over I had read Genesis and Exodus two more times with my daughter. She sat down one evening for the next installment and said, 'Well, Mum, what is God up to tonight?'

"Teaching third and fourth graders in church school was ever so much more enjoyable after I had that first course. Every time I sit down to plan I remember those two questions: Who is God? What are we created to be and do? I want everything we do in class to help us answer those questions."

THE EXAMPLE WE SET FOR CHILDREN

What the narrator of this account does not say is that the answers to the two questions are lifelong quests. Children get clues from teachers and caregivers who persist in their study of scripture in order to know God and our place in the universe.

A four-year-old boy prayed one bedtime with his grandfather, "Come on, God. You can do it. Mom and Dad are mad at each other, and I don't know what to do."

The child's grandfather told the boy it was good to tell

God how he felt about his parents' troubles. "I know God cares about us. I know for certain," the grandfather assured him. Then he read to the child from Philippians 4:4–7, "prayer and supplication with thanksgiving," just as it came from the epistle.

When he finished the child said, "I like to hear you read, Grandpa. I like the part best about 'Now don't you worry about anything, hear?'"

There is no more effective technique for teaching children the importance of the Bible to the church than their witnessing parents, grandparents, teachers, and pastor reading aloud from it. Bible study both sparks and fuels shared ministry. Without it, we may have good works now and then but lack the urgency that comes with an all-out effort to transform the world.

The scriptures are unlike our other books. Generations of men and women of the Book have testified that God speaks to us through the Old and New Testaments.

In a mid-nineteenth-century hymn based on John Robinson's seventeenth-century words to the American Pilgrim families, George Rawson wrote:

> We limit not the truth of God
> To our poor reach of mind,
> By notions of our day and sect,
> Crude, partial, and confined.
>
> No, let a new and better hope
> Within our hearts be stirred:
> The Lord hath yet more light and truth
> To break forth from the Word.

Sing it to the tune of "Our God, Our Help in Ages Past."

One hundred years later Robert McAfee Brown wrote to teenagers about hearing God's voice in Bible study. He suggested that they read scriptures as *actors* in the drama of God's continued reaching out to reclaim all human beings as the people of God. We are not spectators, whether we wish to be or not. The Bible is about us. It is our kind whom

God created and found good in Genesis 1. It is our family who melted earrings and bracelets to make a golden god to do our bidding. It is our ancestors who repented and were baptized on the Day of Pentecost. (And where were we when they crucified our Lord?)

The Bible is indeed our family album.

CHILDREN'S SENSE ABOUT THE BIBLE

Boys and girls take hold of the scriptures in compelling ways. While adults are imploring them to "act like the good Samaritan" and "learn to talk to God the way the boy Samuel did," five-, six-, and seven-year-olds are already being neighbors and praying to God.

Older children tend to test what they hear and read from the Bible. Though sometimes we interpret this behavior as skepticism and doubt, it is very likely closer to wonder and mystery.

Curriculum resources for this age range often employ several steps to getting to the significance of scripture. Though they vary from series to series, here is a basic system in which Bibles and student books are used.

1. The class reads Matthew 22:34–40 and identifies the two commandments as coming from Deuteronomy 6:4–5 and Leviticus 19:18. Someone rereads Matthew 22:40: "On these two commandments hang all the law and the prophets." This step is called, What does the passage (or story) say?

2. The teacher asks, "Where did Jesus learn about the law?" (He grew up in a Jewish family and went to a synagogue school, where he learned to read the law and prophets of the Old Testament.) The class discusses the Pharisees' suspicion of Jesus and his disciples and their wonder at his straight, wise answer. This step is called, What did it mean to the people who were there?

3. The teacher returns to Matthew 22:40 and explains that loving God and our neighbor is our way of being obedient to God. When we worship, we are obedient. When we are thoughtful of others, we are obedient to God's Great Commandment. Everything Jesus did and taught us comes back to the Great Commandment and his obedience to God. The class members learn how to look at portions of scripture throughout the unit in order to test the relationship of the verses to the Great Commandment. The class plans an act of worship and an act of mercy. This step is called, What difference does it make to us today?

Children of two, three, and four respond to the combination of often-repeated sentences in picture books about God, Jesus, and the church. From time to time the teachers' and parents' reading from the Bible reinforces the concept that the stories they know come from the Book of the church.

A woman who teaches a corps of volunteers at a church-run day-care center also coaches a steady stream of Sunday caregivers of toddlers and two-year-olds. She teaches the children as the "cadets" watch. One of the interest centers she introduces as a one-to-one experience is pictures of Jesus posted between the floor and the windowsills. She takes one child by the hand and goes on a mini art tour.

She says very little about each picture. "Jesus is sitting with the children. This fellow looks like you, Adam!"

They go on to another picture. "Jesus is talking to Peter. 'Come with me,' he says. 'Help me with God's work!'"

Then she picks up a Bible from a shelf and sits on the floor to show it to the child. "Look," she says the first time with a child. "This is my Bible, with stories of God and Jesus." She turns to Matthew 19:14. "Jesus told his helpers, 'Let the little children come to me.' What do you think about that?" And the tour is over.

LEARNING ABOUT THE BOOK

It used to be in the eighteenth and nineteenth centuries that parents taught their children how to use the Bible. Some children learned to read with the Bible as their only book. Many children still learn how to use the Bible from adults at church. Some are teaching their parents.

Before young children develop skills in generalizing, Bibles are not always recognizable. Most young schoolchildren know that Bibles come in a variety of shapes, colors, and styles. They can get past the leather, paper, or board covers, the zipper, gilt-edged pages, or thumb index to the title and recognize a Bible. They are curious about the differences from one translation to another and interested in Bibles printed in languages other than English. A concept more difficult to grasp is that their English Bibles came from Hebrew and Greek.

In order to use the Bible, and that is the point of its being in the church, we all need to learn to gain access to it with ease. In shared ministry, those who know teach those who have not learned.

Once a year in October, in a church at the edge of a large city, there are no classes. Everyone plans for and comes to a Bible fair. Each class is given a list of exhibits. Anyone may contribute items such as a Bible in another language, an old Bible, or a Bible that has traveled with its owner. There is always an exhibit of translations of the English Bible. At the most recent Bible fair there was a Revised English Bible (REB) from the United Kingdom and a New Revised Standard Version (NRSV) from the United States. Next to each Bible was an index card with information about the book. On the REB's card it said, *Sent from York, England, by Beatrice Russell, who was an exchange student here in 1985.* On the NRSV's card was written, *The chair of the revision committee was my professor at Princeton Theological Seminary.*

Each children's class teaches something about the Bible to others. At the last fair the "teachers" sat on a platform before an audience.

The three- and four-year-olds began by singing Bible verses from three different translations: King James, Moffatt, and Revised Standard Version. The audience listened and then sang each verse with the class. Many of the adults had never seen a Moffatt translation, much less learned to sing a song from one.

Kindergarten children had drawn transparencies of creation. They showed their story of Genesis 1 on an overhead projector. It was called, "See What God Has Done."

First, second, and third graders played a game with audience participation about testaments, books, chapters and verses of the Bible, and where we find familiar stories.

Fourth, fifth, and sixth graders played "True or false About the Bible." One child was emcee, two had the correct answers, and one had proof. The adults enjoyed the game thoroughly, but a seventh grader prevailed to the end, receiving a button that declared her EXPERT.

The fair comes at the best time of the year for the children, according to the minister.

"In order to prepare for it, they need to learn things they can use over and over during the year. Our fourth graders find references and read with less fuss than their parents."

Curriculum resources usually have Bible skills units in the autumn for children who can read. These units should be kept in the class area throughout the year, so that those who already have mastered the skills may teach those who have not. The object of the skills games and exercises is to make the Bible accessible, so that there is no barrier to its use in the congregation. It may be easier in a class for all to use the same edition of a Bible and refer to page numbers, but students do not learn to do independent Bible study that way. It is far more lasting to learn the idiosyncrasies of the

Book of the church, which is more like a library than a volume of fifteen hundred pages.

CHOOSING CURRICULUM RESOURCES

All mass-produced church education curriculum resources are written, edited, and designed with a viewpoint toward the scriptures, God, Christ, and the church. *Denominationally* produced resources are designed to reflect the viewpoint of the statements of faith and/or creeds of the denomination. *Interdenominational* resources are designed by representatives of the cooperating denominations and based on agreed-upon statements of faith and/or creeds. *Nondenominational* publishers establish their own standards. They may or may not share a denomination's convictions about God, Christ, the scriptures, and the church.

When selecting teaching and learning resources for children it is essential that the persons commissioned by the official board know the beliefs of their denomination. When the school of the church, the preaching, and the lay witness of the congregation reflect consistent biblical beliefs, the congregation and the community are nurtured.

Denominational offices of education in the congregations can be of help in choosing curriculum resources. Some printed assistance may appear to be more detailed than a committee wishes, but it is a place to begin.

A minister of two small village churches asked for volunteers from each congregation to serve as a selection committee. Her hope was to have joint teachers' meetings for Bible study and planning. They began with a printed document from denominational offices. They made progress, but they were impatient. They wanted to "look at material and stop talking about ourselves." The chair of the committee requested help from their conference. A man and a woman came from two nearby churches; they had received training for just this sort of situation.

"They wasted no time," the chair of the committee reported. "They asked us questions we could answer, and we
kept minutes, which we all have copies of. One question
was about what we *expected* of our students. I had never
though about expectations. We all agreed we hoped they
would practice what we taught, but that led us into a discussion where we didn't agree at all!"

The two educators left an assignment for the committee
and came back in two weeks. The committee prepared a list
of what they expected of the learners, teachers, pastor, and
materials. The first statement was: "We need resources that
will help all of us do Bible study as best we can for each age."

At the next meeting the educators introduced teaching
materials to examine in light of the expectations. The committee worked in two teams over a period of two weeks.
One team looked at children's resources, the others at materials for youth and adults. When they came together to report they discovered that they had chosen the same series
for all learners in both churches.

In retrospect, the pastor gives credit to the openness of
the consultants. "But," she remarked, "we had one watch-
dog from Black River who kept us honest. He calls himself a
country lawyer, and people from both churches knew his
style — quiet until he makes a point. He has taught the adult
class ever since he came here fresh from law school in 1956.
He's been in the legislature, and now and then folks urge
him to run for Congress."

A woman who worked on youth and adult selection challenged those who chose the children's materials. She felt a
need for more memorization and much less Old Testament
matter. She told the committee, "We are Christians. The
New Testament is our book."

The lawyer responded, "Grace, I've heard you voice those
objections before, and I'd like to talk them out with you
sometime. But for now, let me put it this way: All the mem-
orizing I did as a kid, I remember doing at home. We read

aloud, heard stories, and had discussions in our classes. The books and quarterlies help the teachers and children get to the meanings of scripture. We can set up our own goals for memorization.

"As for Old Testament stories, I have to disagree with you. The church needs the whole Bible. Jesus was a student of the law and the prophets. He knew them like the back of his hand. If we're considering memorization for our nine- and ten-year-olds, we'd do well to choose some of the passages Jesus quoted from the Old Testament."

The pastor believes that the interest in education in both congregations stems from the hard work of the committee. She leads Bible study about six times during the year. It is intended for teachers, but others from the two churches come as well. She had encouraged the older children in each church to tell stories and do dramatizations with the younger children. With the use of new curriculum resources, the teachers in the two churches plan together and have arranged exchange visits greatly enjoyed by the older children in each church.

The job of choosing educational resources for children is harder rather than easier when the congregation takes the responsibility seriously. It is not a Tuesday-morning agenda item for the minister or ten minutes' worth of discussion at a Christian education subcommittee meeting. Neither is it the right of each teacher to choose resources for his or her class. A curriculum series assures teachers that what they are teaching is part of what the children will be offered as they progress within the system. Teachers may expect of the recommended resources that the designers know how to choose content appropriate to the age groups. They can expect writers and editors to know which teaching and learning techniques are effective and in keeping with the church's understanding of just whose children we all are.

Users of curriculum resources are privileged customers. Especially with denominationally recommended series, teachers, committees, and pastors are encouraged to keep in touch with the designers and editors. They want to know what adaptations the children found enjoyable, what reactions teachers, parents, and pastors had to the teachers' guides. Well documented criticism is of value to revisers and those persons planning teacher education events.

It is helpful to the denomination's educational workers in national and area offices to receive photocopies of letters sent to editorial persons. Knowing your concerns helps them serve everyone better. In shared ministry, it is up to all of us to keep God's purpose for all humankind foremost in our efforts. We are neighbors to men and women at desks in Kansas City, Cleveland, Louisville, Winona Lake, Nashville, Minneapolis, Chicago, and Toronto, to name just a few places.

INTENTIONAL MEMORY BUILDING

As boys and girls repeat verses from the Bible again and again in worship, song, and education about worship, they are assembling a story of scripture that is likely to stay with them through adulthood.

As they hear and read over and over again stories of God's people in the Old and New Testaments, there are ways to make them memorable too. Although much depends on the teachers in the school of the church, the responsibility for memory building belongs to the whole family of God. There are many opportunities for members of the congregation outside of the church school to be instrumental in nurturing people of the Book not yet twelve years old.

The whole congregation needs information about the content and intent of the church school. Many persons not involved in education have never thought of how children learn at two, three, or four years of age. They are unaware of a system supporting the selection of content over the years a school child spends in the elementary grades.

A minister who had served in several churches in Ohio and Indiana wrote brief statements about preschoolers, young school-age children, and middle-school boys and girls in the school of the church. At first he gave them to parents. Then, quite by chance, he left a packet of the folders on a table where volunteers were sending out a mailing.

The woman in charge read the statements and said to the minister when he came in, "We haven't enough of this delightful article about the children." About twenty of them had already been enclosed in envelopes, sealed, and stamped.

"They can't hurt," the minister said to the workers, "but I hadn't intended them to go anywhere."

"Why not?" a retired high school teacher asked. "I never realized until I read your statement just now that I don't remember when I learned what I know about the Bible. I should know that knowledge grows on us from the inside."

Now the folders are in pews, on a browsing table, and where people wait. In the introduction the pastor writes about kindergarten children learning a song that is intended to be the core of all Bible study for the rest of their lives "if we do our work well and systematically for the next ten or so years."

The song is:

You shall love the Lord your God
With all your heart,
With all your soul,
With all your mind.
You shall love the Lord your God.

You shall love your neighbor,
Your neighbor as yourself,
Your neighbor
As yourself.
You shall love the Lord your God.

He goes on to tell of his own daughter in the class asking the teacher, "Ms. Belknap, what's a soul?"

Another child in the class said, "It's in our neck. First heart, then soul, then mind."

"I believe," their teacher said, "that my soul is what God gives me to know I am a person."

" 'I believe,'" the minister concludes, "is an essential part of the system. Our own testimony is one way we answer children's hard questions about God."

When we ask teenagers and adults about their earliest memories of God, Christ, and the church, their answers are not always rooted in the church but almost always related to persons of faith.

In a parents' and teachers' Bible study session, a minister asked about those earliest memories. One man had been born on a Sunday evening after his mother had sung in a church choir concert. He was in church the next Sunday when she sang again. What he likes about his earliest memories is that he knew God was in that place. What he still dislikes is the double standard for children and adults. "I learned Bible verses from men and women who didn't think for one minute about practicing what I was reminded over and over to do."

What verses? He could remember, all right.

"Be kind to one another" (Eph. 4:32). The teacher who taught him that told the class that it was naughty to disagree.

"It is good to give thanks to the Lord, to sing praises to your name." The teacher taught the class to say this before they worshiped. But when the child said, "Let's sing 'Wherever I Go,'" the teacher said, "This is worship; you must be quiet!"

The man grew up around people in the church and his home who could counteract unneighborly teaching, but they could not erase the memory.

A high school senior who assisted in children's music was there with her father. Several times she had tried to interrupt the man, but the minister said, "Kaia, you'll be next."

Then she held forth. "Mr. Blaska, I can't believe we're talking about the same church. Daddy tells me about when I was little, and I think I remember it; but it's hard to know the difference between what you're told and what you know from back there. To me, this church is a place of promises that you trust. I don't think I remember my birth mother. But I know that when I was three I came to this church with my real mother and father, who had adopted me. I only remember loving it here. Once I hit Danny Lowry, and his nose bled. I told him I was sorry right away. But I hit him again, and the teacher—I've forgotten her name—said, 'Sorry isn't enough, Kaia. You have to turn around and not do that anymore. That's the way of God's people, and that's who we all are.'

"You knew you belonged, Mr. Blaska. I wasn't sure if I was one of God's people or not, but I sure did want to be. Then one time in your class you told us what your favorite Bible verse was. That's why I kept interrupting just now. *You* taught about God's promises. I memorized that verse and said it every night in fifth grade before I prayed: 'Once you were no people, but now you are God's people. Once you had not received mercy, but now you have received mercy' " (1 Peter 2:10, RSV).

"What do you think that means, Kaia?" the minister asked.

"You know me," she replied. "What goes in my mind comes out my mouth. It means that nobody, nobody, nobody is on the outside of the people of God. And you know what else it means to me? That my birth mother could run away from me but never from God."

Kaia's father had tears in his eyes. Everyone at the meeting knew that his wife, Kaia's "real" mother, had died two years after Kaia's adoption.

"Kaia tells it like it is. I speak through tears, and I'm not ashamed. But my prized memory is Kaia's ministry to me.

As we trimmed the tree the year after Joanna died, I suddenly filled up with tears.

" 'You're crying, Daddy,' the little tot scolded me.

" 'I know. At times like this I miss your mother a whole lot,' I told her.

" 'Well, don't you think I do too?' she asked.

"She's been teaching me to endure, to speak out in truth and kindness, and to find family in the church. Alex Blaska, this church is a place of promise, and you're one of the reasons."

No congregation is one solid block of intentional memory builders. Double standards in biblical interpretation most likely arise where the Bible itself is misinterpreted. It was never intended as a rule book for outsiders trying to qualify for entrance.

Organizing for Memory Building

The first and foremost principle in working toward lasting, worthwhile memories among the people of God is *inclusiveness*. At Pentecost, Peter told the bewildered crowd:

> Repent and be baptized every one of you in the name of Jesus Christ so that your sins may be forgiven; and you will receive the gift of the Holy Spirit. For the promise is for you, for your children, and for all who are far away, everyone whom the Lord our God calls to him.
>
> —Acts 2:38–39

The present generation of children is likely to take inclusiveness for granted. What boys and girls resent and are most apt to remember are times and places where they were not included. Inclusiveness as an operating principle was never intended to mean that anyone can be anywhere doing anything at any time. It refers to access to the places of learning and worship of God, and acceptance and recognition of God's call to any person of any age or condition.

One Saturday afternoon a horde of humanity advanced upon and filled the sanctuary of a downtown Roman Catholic church for a wedding mass. Outside five boys decided to play with a basketball on the concrete in front of the church. A priest came out of the school building next door. The boys continued their game. He walked over to the playing surface, caught the ball, and slipped it under one arm.

"Do you know what's going on in there?" he asked. They stared at him.

"Yeah, there's a wedding," one finally said.

"You're making a lot of noise out here. The people inside are at worship. It's distracting to hear you shout and to feel the windows shake when the basketball hits the wires."

"You want us to quit playing? Give us back my ball and we'll go where we're welcome," the spokesman told the priest.

"You're welcome on the courts behind the school. We've got baskets out there for you," the priest replied. "After the mass is over and the people have gone you can play here, but I don't know why you'd want to."

He handed the basketball to its owner, and the boys walked slowly to the courts in silence, not even dribbling the ball. A horse and carriage were awaiting the bride and groom. The priest jumped in to chat with the driver.

"I hate telling kids they don't belong," he said.

"You did fine, Father," the driver consoled him. "You gave them a place that's made for playing, and maybe you taught them to think about others."

Thoughtfulness is a learned talent. Those boys and girls who are not reminded in their homes and neighborhoods to regard others as they would be regarded need very much the kind of hospitality the priest offered. Modeling our understanding of biblical teachings reeducates the models as we teach the uninitiated.

Some congregations have put a conscious inclusiveness into their program. Children are seen serving with ushers at the sanctuary door, welcoming "one another . . . as Christ has welcomed you, for the glory of God" (Rom. 15:7). When newcomers are in class for the first time, the veterans vie for the opportunity to "extend hospitality to strangers" (Rom. 12:13).

In a church of nearly four hundred in a town that has had its bouts with unemployment and a mobile population, an after-school child-care group made a Good Samaritan wall display over a period of three months. There were snapshots, original art, and neatly written reports of the activities of the group, with a great number of adult members serving very short terms as advocates. Every activity was a deed of mercy. Every activity had a scriptural base, which was printed in full and posted with the other documents. All activities and Bible verses were related to the Great Commandment, which is the foundation of the parable of the Good Samaritan.

With at least one advocate, the boys and girls, none older than twelve, had visited shut-ins, helped set tables for a meal after a memorial service, gone to sing at the jail, made popcorn balls for the nurses at the hospital, sorted baby clothes for a neighborhood center, packed boxes of food for the emergency cupboard at the church, delivered tapes of the service of worship to a retirement home, and made jack-o'-lanterns for all the children in the hospital. (One even smiled into a window at newborns.)

A woman chose the scripture verses with one of the leaders who was finding community needs. They worked at the woman's apartment, because she was homebound. Several projects were based on verses from Matthew 25:31–46. Other verses were Romans 14:7–9; Galatians 6:10; Philippians 2:4–5.

This program is popular with the children, some of whom were not affiliated with the church before coming to the after-school group. Two of the children were from a family who lived in their aging station wagon when they first

attended. One of the advocates in charge of the babies' lay-
ettes project told of a nine-year-old girl holding up an under-
shirt with *Big Boy* embroidered on it.

"Don't you love it!" she exclaimed. "If our next baby is a
boy, maybe he'll get it!" In shared ministry all of God's people serve their neighbors and are served by them.

Such structured programming involves a great number of
adults and, in this instance, retired persons. Most of the advocates worked for a short time. Young people lent a hand
with the jack-o'-lanterns and helped deliver them. The pattern of short-lived volunteering is a habit now in the congregation. It takes a few well-organized persons to coordinate
and tend the system. The minister told the crowd at a congregational meeting, "This is the first church I've worked in
where the parishioners practice what I preach before I have
time to!"

Where there is no intricately related program of children's biblical education and service in the community, the
intentional memory building still goes on. The essential ingredients are action combined with biblical teaching. We do
not need proof texts before we respond to the cries of the up-
rooted, the starving, or war weary. Those cries are from our
neighbors; those neighbors are all God's people.

The children in our congregations care very much for the
helpless, and they are eager to find ways to help them. All
we need to do is include them in the ministry. Does the
church have a special interest in an overseas mission
project? Let the children write letters to the workers. Do
missionaries visit in the congregation when they are itiner-
ating? Let the children come to see them, ask them questions, and show them around.

A medical doctor who retired after serving many years in
Central Africa always depended on his wife to speak to the
children when they visited supporting churches. After she
died, he ignored the children. At one of the churches that
was engaged in enthusiastic inclusiveness, the children

gathered at his feet as he rose to speak to a roomful of people. He was visibly shaken.

The woman from the congregation who had introduced him stood again and said to him, "Keep calm, Burton. Just talk to us. The children like doctors. They like Africa. But they're hazy about what a missionary is. That's why we want them close."

The "children" included a few preschoolers, about twenty-five in elementary grades, and even more young people. At the question period they asked for more information than the adults did. An eight-year-old child wanted to know, "What do you do when there is a war over there?"

The man said, "I have never been in a war, but I have been close to fighting. I suppose we would take care of the people who were wounded and do the best we could."

"So would I," the child agreed.

Children Teaching Children

In curriculum resources for children there are periodic suggestions for taking a Bible story, a dramatization, or a choral reading of scripture to another class. The purpose is generally for review. In shared ministry we call it "giving the story away." Teaching becomes an integral part of children's learning — learning to tell and show others what they have heard and seen. When it is done often enough and well enough it serves as review for the "teachers" and as learning to another class.

Use the technique described in the curriculum resources. Almost every activity reinforces the learning of a Bible story or scripture study. The activities that travel best are dramatizations, illustrated stories in a pasteboard-box TV set, songs the children can teach others, and scriptural choral speaking. Some teachers regard the visits as interruptions. It is best to take children where they are regarded as the teachers and evangelists they are setting out to be. They should never go anywhere unexpected unless that is the point of the visit. (First graders delivered thank-you cards in a large church building with no warning and no words at all. They went into a room, delivered the card, and left. Each card said *Thank you. Read 1 Thessalonians 1:2–3. The First Grade Class*. The custodians were pleased; some of the teachers were amused; the organist, who was practicing, saw a small hand deliver a yellow card to a keyboard and disappear.)

With sporadic attendance being more the rule than consistent attendance, older children can tutor one another and it is ten minutes well spent. A child who is learning to use the Bible can hone his or her skills by teaching the uninitiated in a one-to-one setting. If a child comes for the first time toward the end of a unit with a continued story, one child can tell it to the other in what is called "catch-up" work, using student books and the Bible. Sometimes the whole class might review an epic such as the exodus, giving a teacher an opportunity to assess the learning of the regular attenders.

A WORD ABOUT THE BOOK

The Bible is our text. God speaks to us as we read and study it. We teach children how to use it and show them by our actions that we continue to read and study it as long as we are able.

But the Bible is a book, not a god. It is God's Word, to be sure; but the Word is older than any book. In the Gospel of John we read that "In the beginning was the Word, and the Word was with God . . . . And the Word became flesh and lived among us" (John 1:1, 14).

As people of the Book we are bearers of the Word. As we teach and as we learn in the church, we are not alone with the Old and New Testaments. God is in us and around us all as we serve one another. It is God we worship: Creator,

Christ, and Holy Spirit. It is in church that we do this, where God may speak to a child who may give insight to a biblical scholar. Or where children may speak their concerns to God in the community of the people of God.

SUMMARY

The scriptures of the Old and New Testaments are the basis for teaching and learning in the church.

Children learn of the centrality of the scriptures in the church by the examples in word and deed of significant adults around them.

An essential part of children's education in the scriptures is the experience of teaching others in the congregation what they have learned.

Curriculum resources for children need to reflect the beliefs of the denomination and be rooted in the scriptures. Choosing resources is a responsibility of the governing body of the congregation.

Planning for intentional memory building involves focusing on congregational experiences in which children and adults cooperate in necessary work to benefit the worship, study, and well-being of others. Children who tutor other children in their own classes are likely to acquire a firm base on which to build memories of the gathered people of God.

3

At Worship in the Congregation

The service of worship is directed to God. The liturgy is the work of the people. It is not an educational opportunity. We may learn as we worship, but our reason to gather with God's people is to worship God who has called us. One thing we may learn is just who God's people are.

In a small congregation in rural Maine during the fall foliage season, the sanctuary was filled. Tourists were surely people of God from elsewhere, or why would they be here? the regulars thought. In the first pew, directly in front of the minister, sat two girls looking to be eight and ten years old. The older one's coat was buttoned wrong, and the younger one's jacket had no buttons at all. They both kicked their shoes off and sat on their bare feet.

One of the members said to her visiting sister, "I wonder who those dirty little girls are!"

As the service progressed, the two girls found it difficult to follow since they were in the front pew. The minister handed them an open hymnal and they sang. Sitting and standing was confusing, but they persevered. When it came time for Communion they turned around and watched the elders distribute the elements. Obviously, this kind of Communion was a new experience for both. When the tiny glasses were passed, the older one held hers up to the light before she drank from it. Then she went to the minister at the Communion table and asked, "Can I pick up them little glasses?"

"Go ahead," the pastor replied, about to hand her a tray.

Instead the child went to each worshiper, collected the glass, and brought it to the tray on the table. It took a long time. The worshipers reacted with amusement at first to see a barefoot child in a crooked coat doing the work of the elders. But her devoutness changed the amusement to awe. (One of the visitors told the pastor after the service that he felt God's presence when he looked at the girl's face.) The worshipers sang the final hymn with more than the usual enthusiasm, and there was a rare display of hospitality between tourists and members on the way out of church.

The pastor's sensitivity to the two children undoubtedly had given the older one the courage to ask if she could clean up. When the elders talked about the incident after worship, one of them said, "They must have known from another church that they would be welcome. Just think, that kid walked around barefoot!"

It took very little time to discover where and in what condition the girls lived. The parish offered the family needed assistance, until one day the house was empty and the girls were seen no more. But while they were there, they were worshiping members in the house of God.

EDUCATION ABOUT WORSHIP

We all need to learn more about why, who, and how we worship, but boys and girls need special coaching before and along with the experience of congregational worship. The first thing they want to know is, "What do we do?" Understandably, they don't want to be uneasy, embarrassed, or laughed at. But that is not enough. Their education begins when they come to church. It continues when they see others of all ages going into the sanctuary.

How Young Children Learn About Worship

A three-year-old boy, new to the child-care workers, viewed his surroundings with suspicion.

"Where'd my dad go?"

"He's in church."

"I'm in church. I want to see my dad."

"Well, he's at worship."

"I want to go to the war ship."

"Worship, Cary. Worship."

"Worship. I want to go."

The teenager talking with Cary said to an adult, "I think I'll take him for a walk to the sanctuary, OK?"

The two left. She told him that he had to be very quiet where they were going. She asked if he knew how to whisper, and he did. She said, "You and I might whisper, but not very often."

They walked into the rear of the silent sanctuary. Cary looked all around. Suddenly they heard the organ, and the people stood up to sing. The teenager took Cary's hand and walked down one side of the room until his father spotted them. He came out of the pew.

"What's up?" he asked.

"You have to whisper, Dad," Cary whispered.

"We're just visiting. He wanted to see where you went," the caregiver told him. Then to Cary she said, "Come on. Let's go back and see what the other kids are doing."

"Bye, Dad," Cary whispered, and waved. On the way to the nursery he asked, with a wrinkled-up nose and puzzled expression, "What do they do in that worship?"

"They sing and pray to God. The minister talks," the teenager said. Cary seemed to be satisfied.

A slightly older child might sit in the service of worship for a short time and then go to child care. It is important to young children's understanding of the service of worship that they build mental images of the activity in the sanctuary. It also helps them worship, in their own mysterious way, to see all sorts, sizes, and ages of people gathered to sing praises, hear scripture read and taught, and be present as sacraments are administered.

Children of three, four, and five vary greatly in their interest and ability to participate in worship. Coming in to sit or stand for a short time in order to hear singing is a good start. Witnessing a baptism up close or listening to the reading of scripture might happen on subsequent Sundays. Looking around the sanctuary when there is no service introduces them to the special furniture, adornments, and tools of worship. When they stand at a pulpit or lectern they get the opposite view of the room from what they see from a pew. Looking closely at a large Bible and at a pew Bible, handling a hymnal, examining communion ware, baptismal font, and chancel furnishings, all inform their participation in worship from then on.

After attending one portion of the service, it is instructive to concentrate on another ten- or fifteen-minute segment of the worship hour. Festival days and special services are often positive experiences if young children are prepared for what to expect.

The schoolchildren in a parish in England give the rest of the congregation a Sunday morning Advent service each year. One of them had a dramatization in which nativity characters came through the sanctuary looking for the Christ child. Children of five and under were dressed in sweaters and stocking caps and sat on the chancel steps, watching the congregation and the activity in the aisle. The teenager with them knew that if a child grew tired or restless she could let him or her set out to find a parent. No one moved. When the carolers came up the aisle and said, "Come on, let's go to the manger," the little crew went willingly.

Those children had never known a time when they were not welcome in the sanctuary. Although many adults did not know them by their Christian names, they knew their surnames and often their grandparents. The presence of familiar adults and parents at such events lessens the responsibility for early orientation by others in the church. But the job of education for worship needs to come from those adults and young people who know that all services of worship are directed to God. When children are up in front they are not performing for an audience. They are leading the congregation in worship.

Assisting in worship is what children's choirs are intended to do. Directors of church music prefer to keep very young children's singing groups as learning choirs until they are able to assist in worship. Parents and other appreciative worshipers may work at cross-purposes with a director's educational aims. Applauding young children for singing an introit may be an innocent reaction to a job well done, but it focuses on the performer instead of the object and act of worship. Pressing the director to let the youngest children sing before they know how to sing together may result in a comic performance but not in any way a "joyful noise to the Lord." Education for worship needs to go on for all members, not just children.

Preschoolers are beginners in every way they relate to congregational worship. There is no need to press the abstractions of worship upon them. They are not ready to discuss praise and prayer, but they can sing praises and pray with others. Neither is it necessary to make the service of worship an endurance contest.

As a mother of five children counsels mothers of infants, toddlers, and preschoolers, "Take the children out before they get restless. They are more likely to want to keep coming to church with you." She says that she and her husband took great pride at attending mass with their children until they had four, the oldest being ten.

"Our two-year-old son was not as interested as the others had been in looking, listening, and imitating the rest of us. His ten-year-old sister used to take him for walks and come back in after the homily. One Sunday he sat contentedly at the end of the pew.

"At last! I said to myself. He's caught up in worship. When we were out in the parking lot, I picked him up to buckle him in his seat. His legs were covered with the cursive penmanship of his oldest sister—black, fine-line, felt-tip ink.

" 'Maurine!' I cried.

" 'He loved it, Mom,' she explained. 'It tickled.' "

Teenagers and older elementary school children do well on short assignments with young children at worship. But if no one coaches them, we can expect some lapses in judgment.

A woman who is likely to be teaching a Bible study for adolescents one Sunday and caring for babies the next tells of an unrecognized service some middle-school children perform during worship.

One Sunday there were seven of these boys and girls begging to help her in child care, name tags already pinned on.

She said, "Mandy and I need only two of you. Decide who's going to stay, and the rest of you go to worship."

"Oh, Mrs. McKay, that's boring," one moaned. "Please let us stay!"

She refused, but she had a suggestion. "There are new families in our church with rambunctious toddlers and two-year-olds. I guess the parents have been taught that the children should be in church. When they cry and shout and kick, their parents are embarrassed, but they don't take them out.

"Now, here's my plan. You go into the sanctuary and sit next to one of those families. Introduce yourself and establish eye contact with the child. When the boy or girl starts a floor show, you say to the parents, 'Pardon me. Would you like me to take the baby for a walk? We'll meet you right here after the service.' If they say no, stay there; chances are they'll change their minds.

"This is a tricky situation. You see, if I asked them they might think, That *woman* is trying to tell us not to bring our children to church. If an usher told them where the child-care room is they might think, This *church* doesn't want children in worship. That isn't true. We want them to like being there.

"But if you go in one by one and offer to help, those parents will smile and say, 'Now, aren't you sweet?'

"OK. Go in there and be sweet."

Five losers, as they called themselves, went on their mission. In ten minutes or so one came back with an unsteady walker in a sailor suit and hat. Another followed with a girl clutching a velour tiger. He reported that a third was circling with two children.

"When you return them to their parents tell them about our room. Offer to sit with them again if they wish," the woman told them.

After worship the two unemployed nannies returned complaining of contented children. Mrs. McKay listened and then said, "Come back next week and try again." They have. It isn't a program of the church—just a few young people who want little children to like being there.

Older Children Learn, Worship, and Teach

When boys and girls begin to read, education for worship takes on a new dimension. They can learn to use the tools of worship—hymnals, pew Bibles, books of worship, and orders of service.

A good many congregations offer that kind of learning to the children at the hour of congregational worship. The boys and girls gather in the sanctuary for about twenty minutes of the service and then leave for classes. This is not basic instruction in Bible. That either precedes or follows worship. When the congregation gathers at one hour for education and at another to worship God, no adult need give up worshiping for the school year in order to be teaching.

In shared ministry the teachers of children in worship education are at first adults, then young persons and adults, and, in a few instances, as time and education go on, older children, young people, and adults. No one teaches for more than four or five sessions of clearly focused work.

A Tutorial Model

A congregation in the Southwest created a shared ministry model of worship education by trying to offer a program borrowed from a nearby church. Two instructors offered short units to teach young people and children how to read and use the printed order of service. The teachers soon determined that what middle and high school students learned in two half-hour sessions, the third-grade boys and girls could hardly learn at all before being taught how to use a hymnal and the pew Bible.

The young people volunteered to tutor the children in the class. They sat together in worship until the hymn before the sermon. Then they all went to class. The attendance of both tutors and learners was unpredictable, but it became more consistent as responsibilities were redefined.

One of the original instructors recalls that he told three tutors fresh from the sanctuary, "You have the next three Sundays to do your stuff, whether you're here or not. If we just taught in the church when the teachers felt like coming, we'd all grow up to know nothing."

"But what if our pupils don't show up?" an eighth-grade girl asked him.

"Call them. Tell them there's a beginning and an end to your offer."

The tutors took the mild scolding as a challenge. Attendance improved immediately. After the three-week course the original instructors taught the broadly graded group about the acts of worship as they occur in the service of worship in their own congregation. One of the instructors, a physical education teacher, noted that the combination of attending worship and learning about it in sessions immediately following was "efficient education." She observed that "the students' interest is high and their questions relate to our common experience. We have developed team spirit in a little over a month."

The minister is encouraged by the interest of the class. Not only are there more young people and children interested in the worship of God, their parents are attending services as well.

During the unit on the acts of worship the instructors found that the tutors were eager to continue their one-to-one or small-group teaching. The young people were able to familiarize the children with the order of service, and the instructors spent their time on content. After two sessions a high school tutor suggested that they attend a portion of the service other than the first twenty minutes. One of the instructors brought the request to the minister.

"Jonathan"—the minister sighed—"think about your question. Do you have to *ask* the pastor if you can come to church?"

The class decided to come in during the hymn before the sermon. The minister gave them a brief outline of the sermon and portions of scripture to read before attending.

Tutors and their students continued to sit together after the unit was finished. Two more persons led them in a unit on the sacraments. Following that, they wrote prayers and a litany of praise in three sessions with a writer in the congregation. The litany was incorporated in the service of worship with a note elsewhere in the bulletin thanking the class for the contribution.

The minister claims that what the congregation is doing to educate worshipers is a model only for what the education committee will plan next year. Other churches have asked for help, and he invites the inquirers to visit and talk with the designers. The resources they use are denominational. The sequence of units and tutorial methods are a consequence of knowing the learners and their needs.

Adopting approaches and even unit outlines from other

churches is often an effective way to begin worship education. Using denominational resources is instructive to leaders who may need the background. Ultimately, though, the design that fits the particular group of learners has been adapted before and during its use. Before it is used another year with another group it will probably need to be adapted again. Interest, parental support, attendance, and capacity to learn are only a few factors that make one group of children and young people different from the next.

Be a Friend and a Teacher

A retired Air Force officer and his wife spend summers in a northern resort area where the population multiplies from five hundred to a total of ten thousand in season. Attendance at the village churches increases dramatically from June through August. The couple lost no time in getting involved in the leadership of the congregation. During coffee time after worship one Sunday, the man remarked to the pastor and an usher, "The adults in this church don't know a stranger. Very friendly place. But I'd like a crack at teaching the eight- to ten-year-olds how to welcome other children. Marge and I sat by two village kids who sang, prayed, and found the Bible lessons. They could be hosting some of there other children who sit like bumps on logs next to their parents."

"Go ahead, Herb." The pastor laughed. "We trust you to get results." Results came quickly. Herb phoned a few children during the week and invited them to the house for hot dogs and picnic fare. They were glad to come. Even with an exploding population around them there are not many surprises for eight- to ten-year-olds in a northern village surrounded by forests and cold, deep fishing lakes.

In Herb's report to the deacons he said, "I told the five children about my work at each of the base chapels when I was in the Air Force. Families were coming and going as a way of life. Every child in my church school classes was expected to be a friend and a teacher when new children came. Sometimes they had hardly learned anything themselves before they were reaching out in friendship to someone else. We had children of divorced parents who came for brief periods of time, children who were transferred with their families, and very few of that age who stayed two years. And we had those who left because their parents split up, along with all the others whose folks had orders to other bases.

"When they came to worship the first time the children greeted them at the sanctuary door. 'I'd like to sit with you this morning,' a class member would say. They shared the hymnal and the pew Bible. If the Lord's Supper was being celebrated, the class member led the way.

"I asked the village children if they could be friends and teachers to the summer boys and girls. I told them they had to go into training, and they agreed to it. We started right away."

The next week the five village children stood at the door. Four of them extended their hands in fellowship and sat with visitors near their own age. The fifth child, a fourth-grade boy, served as an usher of three other children.

"Hi," he said. "I'm Kyle Lollier. Would you and your parents like to meet my class after worship? We want to get to know you."

Herb made an announcement in the service for eight- to ten-year-olds and their parents to meet after the service.

Each week during the summer the village children sought out summer children who were staying anywhere from a week to two months. Midweek they met with Herb and Marge for a picnic. There were always at least ten and once seventeen eight- to ten-year-olds. The village children began collecting postcards from visitors who had gone home. One said, "That's the first time I ever had fun in church."

At the end of the season the children helped the deacons

host a party for Herb and Marge. One of the older children wondered what she could do next year when she wouldn't qualify for the group.

"Start one of your own," Herb told her. She plans to do just that.

The pastor and deacons assumed that the village boys and girls had learned to offer instant hospitality, serving as teachers to children in unfamiliar surroundings. They were pleased with the outcome of Herb's "crack" at the eight- to ten-year-olds. When church school resumed in the autumn the superintendent asked the five to report to the whole school. She asked questions of individuals, and others made comments.

Q: How did you feel on the first Sunday?

A: Col. Grayson showed us what to do, and we practiced beforehand. I hoped everything would be fun, and it was.

Q: What did you learn from your work in the church?

A: I didn't really learn anything. What is different, though, is how much I like to go to church. When you teach other people what to do, you pay more attention.

COMMENT: You really, really do. Like when Pastor Kern said Jesus showed us how to be human, of all things. I never thought that was so great, but it is.

Q: What is the best thing you remember?

A: There was this Ricky in his wheelchair, and his parents said he could hang on to me and his dad and walk up to take Communion. That was the goodest.

Q: How do you think the summer children felt?

A: That's hard. The ones who stayed the longest, like Lori and Ab, liked the picnics. There's nothing to do here if you don't have friends and books.

Teachers of Parents

Since restrictions have been lifted on emigration of Jews in the Soviet Union, thousands of families have come to the United States. The largest share are settling in New York City, and the rest across the country in San Diego, Atlanta, Baltimore, and twenty or more other cities where Jewish congregations welcome them.

The children are often given places in yeshivas and academies, where they learn the Hebrew alphabet and study their heritage. In a Youngstown, Ohio, academy fourteen Soviet children were admitted on full scholarships. In New York there are five schools just for immigrants, preparing them for yeshiva education in a year or two.

These children are absorbing what their parents may never have learned or may remember from a grandparent long ago. The children go home and teach what they are learning. They interpret the customs, rites, and festivals to uninitiated parents. Some are receptive; some are not. The children are claiming their status as people of God. They are learning for the first time story upon story of who the God of Abraham, Isaac, and Jacob is and how that God continues to bless the worshiping people.

> I will surely gather all of you, O Jacob,
> I will gather the survivors of Israel;
> I will set them together
> like sheep in a fold,
> like a flock in its pasture;
> it will resound with people.
> —Micah 2:12

A suburban couple were in what they now call self-imposed exile from their church when they adopted seven-year-old Greg. Within the last year both man and woman have become regular worshipers and dependable leaders—because of their son.

For a whole year they took him to church school, but

they did not attend themselves. They both worked long hours, they reasoned, and didn't have time. The next year they took him to choir rehearsals but rarely came to worship when the choir sang. When the new pastor arrived, he urged the children to be in congregational worship week by week. Greg accepted the invitation. He talked very little about what went on but, according to his mother, seemed comfortable about being at church. The longer the parents stayed away, the more they postponed attending worship.

Finally, the day Greg was nine years old they all went to Sunday morning worship. He sat erect and proud between his parents. Before the service began he put markers in their hymnals and in the pew Bibles. He wrote at the top of each bulletin, *means stand up.* He was attentive during the sermon.

One evening early in the week that followed, the pastor telephoned and asked when he could call. Not until he visited did the parents discover that Greg had filled out a card saying *Mr. and Mrs. Paul Arturi would like a call from the minister.*

The whole family enjoyed the visit, and the parents assured the pastor of their return to worship. He told them that their enthusiasm would encourage Greg in his ministry.

"The people of God at work and worship at Centenary are of all ages," he told them. They knew this already. One of them was nine.

It has never been the children's responsibility to bring their parents to God. That is God's work. But having, as the pastor called it, a "ministry" is the vocation of every one of God's people.

DAYS AND SEASONS IN THE CHURCH YEAR

The calendar in the church is one way of keeping all of us focused on Jesus Christ. The church year is divided into days and seasons that order our worship in relationship to the life of Jesus and the effect his life has on God's people.

Young children often confuse Jesus and God. Older children are bewildered by our explanations of the Trinity. It helps them to know that we all grow in faith as we search for understanding. We do not wait until children understand the Christ before encouraging them in Christian worship with the people of God. That would indeed be a restriction barring all of us from the Lord's table. We invite them to share the mystery with us.

The days and seasons observed in worship in the church inform us of the biblical accounts of Jesus and the people of God. The scriptures speak to us and leave us with new insights. The faith of children in search of understanding can be a model for adult believers.

Christian churches vary in the detail given to their calendars; however, the outline is this:

- *Advent* is a season to remember the Old Testament hopes and prophecies of the coming of Christ and to live in the expectation of the Lord's coming again.
- *Christmas* is a time to celebrate the birth of Christ.
- *Epiphany* is a day to praise and thank God for showing us in human form what it means to be created in the image of God. In the weeks that follow we read and hear of the compassionate ministry of Jesus to all people.
- *Lent* is a season of preparation for our celebration of the death and resurrection of Christ. Children sometimes call it the Road to Easter. The scriptures remind us of the events in the life of Jesus after "he set his face to go to Jerusalem" (Luke 9:51).
- *Holy Week* is a time in which we remember the last days of Jesus with his disciples, celebrate the Lord's Supper, and hear again of his suffering and death.
- *Easter* is a day and a season when we rejoice in the

good news of Christ's resurrection. The scriptures remind us of his work before his ascension and the witness of the believers in the early church.

- *The Day of Pentecost* is a time when the worshiping people of God celebrate the coming of God's Spirit to the whole church.

The church year is known worldwide. As we gather to worship in Helena, Eureka, or Biloxi, God's family members in Seoul, Perth, and Frankfurt have already sung hymns of thanksgiving for God's coming in Jesus Christ. We are an *ecumenical* household of faith. (The Greek root *oikos* means "house.")

An American couple and their ten-year-old daughter were in new Delhi, India, on the third Sunday of Advent. The man was on sabbatical from a state university. For three months the woman and child had been soaking up the culture in Nepal and India. As Christmas approached they all found themselves longing for home, which was still three months away. A friend of the family had given them advice about spending Christmas in a country where Christianity claims a small minority of the worshipers.

She had said, "Go to church. The Church of North India will welcome you. It has roots in so many denominations, you'll fit right in."

The church they found was near the embassies in the capital city. When they arrived they were surprised to see the sanctuary full of people. An usher informed them they were at the service in Hindi. "The next service is in English," he said, "but you are welcome to this one if" — and he chuckled — "you can find room." Not wanting to miss anything on her father's sabbatical, the daughter found seats in the rear, and they witnessed a baby's baptism by sprinkling. The baby's parents were surrounded by at least a dozen adults.

The English service was informal by the family's standards. Children were dismissed to classes just before the sermon.

"Britt," the American woman whispered to her daughter, "do you want to go to a class?"

With no hesitation the child went out. When she returned, her parents were in conversation with the minister. He was an English Baptist, he told them. The congregation had been Baptist before the Church of North India was formed. As he spoke, a third horde of people were coming to worship in the Tamil language.

"And you enjoyed yourself at Sunday school, did you?" the pastor said to Britt.

"I sure did," she replied with her best Missouri twang. "Singing Christmas carols was like coming home to me."

At lunch the three talked about the events of the morning.

"You wouldn't believe that Sunday school!" Britt exclaimed. "I talked to kids from—here, I'll show you." She took a notebook from her jacket pocket. She had asked the boys and girls for autographs and had found out they too were from far away. "From five continents," she bragged, "and a bunch of islands." Her father looked at the children's names: Ukaegbu, Chienda, Siballa, Mburu, McKenzie, Malouf, Forecast, Wong, Yamaya.

"We sang carols, Daddy. And we all knew some of them, and some of us sang different ones besides, while the rest sang along."

"What did you teach them?" her mother asked.

" 'Il Est Né,' " she answered.

"But honey, that's French," her mother told her.

"Who cares? It's been my favorite since second grade."

"Britt," her father said, "the minister mentioned in his sermon that Christians 'come home' at Christmas in the churches of the world. I believe that, after this day."

"Me too, Daddy!"

PARTICIPATION IN WORSHIP

Why is it that children in one congregation flock to the sanctuary and in another find any excuse to avoid congregational worship? The answer may have to do with their preparation, the expectations of parents, teachers, and clergy, or the service itself. What is done in the name of worship needs to be geared to the congregation. In a nursing home it probably is inappropriate to sing "Rise up, O Saints of God" or "We Thank you, Lord, for Strength of Arm." Likewise when there are lively children in a service of worship, they might respond to the Word in active ways that assist others in worship. Such involvement assures them of their membership in the community and reminds other people of the ministry children are able to perform.

Here are several significant ways children have participated in a Sunday service.

1. Commissioning for Service to the Community. Boys and girls ages eight through twelve in the center of a northern New England township met on Wednesday afternoons in the barn adjoining the minister's house. Their loose organization was called Club. They had Bible study and project time. Most of the projects were out in the community—raking leaves for someone who was not able; scrubbing Second Chance, the used clothing outlet; helping at the recycling center and collecting newspapers.

One afternoon the Bible study was Luke 10:1–12, 17, the story of Jesus sending out the seventy, two by two. Two girls began talking about visiting townspeople two by two. The minister was not totally convinced they could or should visit without an adult.

"How about if we talk to people in their gardens or on their porches?" one of the girls asked. "We could go now and try it."

"I'll talk to the deacons," the minister told them, "and let you know in a couple of days."

On Sunday after the sermon four pairs of children were commissioned for Wednesday afternoon community hospitality. In the sermon the pastor had said that the children of Club had responded to the Word and asked for the privilege of visiting people in their gardens and on their porches.

"I believe," he said, "that God is calling these boys and girls to a work of compassion."

In the commissioning service the children promised to be peacemakers and to report to the congregation.

2. Bringing Offerings. One Great Hour of Sharing banks are popular with young children. It is a Lenten offering box for hunger relief, self-development of people, and emergency aid. Some families keep the bank near where they eat, remembering the hungry with part of their food allowance. On the Sunday when adults bring their envelopes of One Great Hour offerings, children in many congregations bring their banks to the chancel.

Older children often prize the opportunity to learn the delicate arts of ushering and taking the weekly offering from worshipers to chancel.

3. Remembering Someone Who Has Died. One of the most difficult experiences for children, teachers, and pastor is the untimely death of one of the boys or girls. When congregation and family are grieving, the children welcome something to do. Occasionally, an older child will have a suggestion, but it is healing for a class to be given a choice of ways to remember their contemporary.

After an eleven-year-old boy shot himself while playing with a deer rifle, the church school superintendent and pastor in a rural congregation gave the children these options: Make a list of what we want to remember about Matt and write a prayer of thanks for his life; put a book in our lending library; plant a tree out by the fireplace in his memory.

They chose to make the list. Matt was a fighter who

stuck up for little kids. He wasn't afraid of much. He was a good runner. He knew so much about fishing he taught things to adults. He wanted to be a ranger when he grew up.

They wrote a prayer of thanks on sheets of newsprint. When they read it a second time, a second-grade boy stood up and said to the teacher, "It isn't right. We have to say to God that we're going to miss him around here." The prayer became a litany. Three children read the leaders' parts, and the congregation prayed in unison: "We're going to miss him around here, God."

4. Reading Correspondence. Reading is talent enough to bring to worship. When children can read aloud effortlessly and communicate the meaning, they can learn to read in worship. One of the coveted responsibilities in an old downtown church in the South is the reading of missionaries' correspondence. There are men and women in the congregation who remember not only the first time they read such letters, but they know the names and work of the missionaries as well.

A visiting relative sat next to a nine-year-old girl during the reading by a boy a year or two older. The girl whispered, "I'm being coached to read now. I can hardly wait."

To participate in this way, it is important to do good work. Coaching takes very little time and uses an older Christian's ability to enable a younger one to act.

5. Taking Part in the Sacraments. Whether or not children are participating in Baptism or the Lord's Supper, they need to be close enough to see and hear what is going on. In some congregations young children are invited to come to the chancel and witness the baptism of infants. Older children occasionally surround one of their classmates who is being baptized.

As the Lord's Supper is celebrated, children need to sit with persons who know what to do. Small variations in the rite can confuse and embarrass a child. This is a valid ministry for adults and young people. Church school and education for worship classes are appropriate places to learn about the sacraments.

6. *Assisting in Worship Through Music.* Children's vocal groups and bell choirs give many older boys and girls valid responsibilities in worship. The years spent in children's choirs are memorable. Men and women in Bible study groups marvel at the amount of scripture they remember from children's choir anthems of days gone by. Boys and girls who do not choose to sing and come to rehearsals can sometimes be encouraged to participate in special services with rhythm instruments and signing for the deaf and partial-hearing members.

Choir members are often willing to teach hymns and responses to others in church school or education for worship. All schoolchildren who attend worship eventually learn the Doxology, Gloria Patri, or choral responses special to their congregation. Choir members might well be intentional about teaching service music to their classmates.

A WORD ABOUT CHILDREN'S TALKS AND SERMONS

"Junior" sermons were part of Protestant church culture in America fifty or more years ago. (They were less common in the British Isles.) They fell into disuse and disfavor, but a "children's time" has resurfaced and is now a part of many services in a wide range of denominations. A minister conversing with and telling stories to the children is engaged in pastoral work. If he or she uses such opportunities in order to get to know the boys and girls, the service of worship is a most unlikely place in which to reach that goal.

Those men and women in pastoral ministry who are more at ease talking with small groups of children similar in age know the value of the relaxed give-and-take in conversation without a backdrop of older worshipers. The difficulties of conversing in a service of worship relate to children's being heard by the congregation and the minister being understood by so wide an age range as two through eleven years. Telling a story without conversing may appear to solve a problem, but it creates another serious one. Children under seven or so perceive language literally. Trying to explain a metaphor or simile is both a waste of time and the beginning of colossal misunderstanding about God, Christ, and the church. (Camels going through eyes of needles, logs in eyes, living water, and stones crying out?) One of the reasons we have age-group classes in the school of the church is to get acquainted with the stories and language of the scriptures in ways appropriate to the boys' and girls' human development.

A teacher of second and third graders in an inner-city church is a former kindergarten teacher from the nearest public school. She plays an occasional game of "I Used to Think" with her class, telling the children about some "used-to-thinks" of five- and six-year-olds she taught. During the games children learn from other children's insights.

One time she told the class about the kindergartners who thought the voices on the intercom came from heaven. They laughed heartily.

An eight-year-old boy told about his high school brother convincing him on the way home from church that the squeak of the faulty fan belt in the family car was the "still, small voice of God."

"My brother was telling me that God was coming after me and was under the hood right then. Finally my mom told him to stop. But in the Bible, God really speaks to people somehow."

"Sure," one of the second graders said, "but how could God squeeze under the hood of your car with all that other stuff in there?"

The oldest child in the class, a sedate nine-year-old girl, spoke up. "My grandma says God is a spirit and can be everywhere at once, not like us with bodies. God would not have to hide in your car at all. A spirit might be—yeah, that's it. God's Spirit is on my ear, and I hear something I have to do. Then the Spirit is on my lips, and I say something just right."

"And on your legs and you go somewhere," another girl added.

The teacher said, "Remember the song you all learned in Downtown Bible School last summer? Our conversation reminds me of "Gracious Spirit, Dwell with Me."

"Gracious Spirit, dwell with me;
I myself would gracious be;
And with words that help and heal
Would your life in mine reveal;
And with actions bold and meek
I for Jesus Christ would speak."

This kind of conversation is best held without adult worshipers listening and without the leader being concerned about its taking time from something else in the order of worship.

When children come forward in the sanctuary to hear a story just for them, they assume it is in their language. There are hundreds of stories of children's misinterpretations of what they learned in church. Some are told by persons whose teachers were on hand to help. Many are told by teachers who did the decoding. We don't hear from everyone. We don't know what misinterpretations are still unexamined. In this day of children in joint custody, in a series of foster homes, or in an unfamiliar country, the church serves children by knowing them individually, including them as active worshipers, inviting them to learn in the school of the church, and taking time with a few to talk and tell stories.

Children who are receiving education for worship and participating in worship are occupied with activities that focus on God as the object of worship. They are busy as they praise, pray, read, and listen. Adults may miss hearing a children's sermon or chat. The pastor may have to rethink his or her sermon preparation if the complaint comes from many. Perhaps other members than children would profit from education for worship.

SUMMARY

Education for worship accompanies participation in worship. Adults and young people may assist children in short-term units and projects.

Older children and youth, upon learning to use the tools of congregational worship, may tutor other children in their use.

With adult help, schoolchildren can extend hospitality to visiting children during a service of worship.

Children today are sometimes faced with teaching their families about congregational worship.

The church year is a useful reminder of the content of worship in relation to the life and ministry of Jesus.

There are significant ways that children with adult help can occasionally take leadership responsibilities in congregational worship.

4

"A Multitude Keeping Festival"

These things I remember,
 as I pour out my soul:
how I went with the throng,
 and led them in procession to the house of God,
with glad shouts and songs of thanksgiving,
 a multitude keeping festival.
> —Psalm 42:4

Festivals in the church are designed to be memorable. They are planned by two generations, recalled by a third, and remembered in story by later ones.

Before the tenth anniversary of a church in the Southwest, the planning committee asked members to tell them what they remembered about ground breaking, cornerstone laying, and dedication ceremonies. The chair of the committee summarized the findings by saying that he wasn't sure the people were reporting on the same events or even from the same church.

One memory survived all filters and was verified on videotape. At the dedication of the building, the architect, builder, and bishop were at the front of a procession when suddenly a tiny boy darted from the crowd, pursued by his sister. The bishop picked up the toddler, the builder hoisted the girl onto his shoulders, and the children were the first to set foot in the dedicated building. When the bishop spoke later in the day, he said, "Remember this day. Tell your children about it. The time may come again to God's people

when we cherish our memories as a remnant people, oppressed, and scattered. Now we are a multitude keeping festival."

Celebrations in the church have reasons for being. The
more focused we remain on the reason, the more memorable the occasion is likely to be. Significant participation by
children needs preparation, support during the event, and
evaluation. In some traditions, boys and girls are provided
with a secondary feast to keep them amused and away from
the primary reason for celebrating. In congregations where
children are regarded as members who share in the ministry, they can assist in substantial ways.

There are two kinds of festivals in Christian congregations, those celebrating the church year and those relating
to milestones in the life of a congregation, denomination, or
institution. Although worship may be part of any celebration, it may not be the primary reason for assembling.

A third kind of celebration is one to which we are invited
by people of other faiths and for which we may need special
preparation.

No one congregation spends its energies and resources on
a steady diet of church feasts. Every service for the Lord's
Day is a festival at which we remember the life, death, and
resurrection of Jesus Christ. But over a period of ten years a
congregation might plan two or three celebrations each year
apart from what is normally scheduled for the Lord's Day.
These festal days are often long in the planning, involving
the talents of many in the church and community. Hymns
may be written and music composed. Guests may need to
know details long in advance. Children's singing and instrumental groups need time for rehearsing and becoming performing ensembles.

Leadership of special days can appropriately go to persons
not presently shouldering major responsibilities. They may
be former officers and teachers in the church or men and
women who are accustomed to coordinating events in their

workday life. Persons with experience directing or producing plays and musicals have useful talents. In congregations where shared ministry is a way of life, clergy persons know the importance of supporting the chosen leadership of special events. It is also important to keep consulting with them so that everyone is clear about the purposes. Sometimes specialists need the help of clergy in learning how to relate to persons as neighbors. A minister may need to attend planning committee meetings rather consistently to see that responsibilities are delegated and carried out. Teaching the chair of a committee the skills in agenda building, for example, may eliminate mounting disorganization. By the time children are involved it is essential that the directions they receive are clearly known to all leadership.

FESTIVALS OF THE CHURCH YEAR

The church year is marked by holidays whether we keep festivals or not. The celebrations described here are all home grown and might be adapted to other congregations where children are learning that they have a place "with the throng" in the house of God.

Advent

Each year, in a congregation of about a hundred in northwest England, Advent brings exquisite decorations to the sanctuary, a large tree in the schoolhouse, and a Sunday morning service of worship led by the children and young people. During the rest of the year shared ministry is taken for granted by officers and pastor.

When the church school teachers proposed to the elders a project resulting in the buying of a bicycle for a missionary pastor in Madagascar, they would have been willing to work on it by themselves. It drew high interest from the elders, who wanted scout troops and all adult members involved.

But the leadership remained in the church school. The logic was simple: The elders were responsible for the Christian Aid offering, the scout troops perpetuated the toys for tots collection, one man took charge of collecting used foil to support a community project of guide dogs for the blind, and everyone contributed to each.

A woman from another church spoke in a service of worship after she had visited Madagascar. She fueled the children's enthusiasm and pricked the consciences of young people and adults. Not only did the pastor need a bicycle; paper and pencils were so treasured that what we call wastepaper went to school, and a pencil was passed around in class.

The Advent service was planned by the teachers and a woman who wrote and directed the children's comings and goings. After the lighting of the third Advent candle, a girl of nine began a narration. As she read Micah 5:2, the prophet came from the congregation to find out from her what had happened since he wrote those words.

She gave him a hymnal and invited him to "stay, watch, listen, and worship God." As the young people read scripture, the children played the roles of the nativity story. The prophet received the gifts from the shepherds and placed them on the communion table—wreaths of foil, potpie tins, and toys for tots. The wise men, coming from afar, brought money for Christian Aid, unused paper, a bag of pencils, and a white bicycle.

The congregation sang familiar carols throughout. The prophet, who had come with no tangible gift, was urged by the narrator to come to the manger with everyone else.

"Have we not just sung, 'What can I give him? Give my heart'?" she scolded.

He asked, "Just how do you give your hearts here at Woodlands?"

The congregation sang in reply, "Awake, Awake to Love and Work." The minister pronounced the benediction and the congregation adjourned to the schoolhouse, led by shepherds and wise men bearing gifts. There they found Mary, Joseph, and Jesus. They knelt and worshiped while an elder led the men and women in singing "O Come, All Ye Faithful."

Christmas

At a conference in Cyprus for Christian writers, editors, and publishers from five continents and the South Pacific, the most frequent request for help was in the area of worship resources for children. There was a publisher as young as twenty-five and a writer in her seventies. Much of what these adults remembered from their own childhood was missionary-led worship, singing, and Sunday school for the children. The one time they remembered being with adults and participating was for a Christmas pageant, but most did not associate the event with worship.

With a representative committee the conference leadership created "Christmas in September." They planned a service of worship around the nativity accounts in the Gospels of Luke and Matthew. The community was invited and children from the town of Ayia Napa played the parts of Mary, Joseph, Jesus, angels, shepherds, and wise men.

Because English was the language of the three-week conference, the order of service was printed in English. All scriptural selections were read in the language of the reader. Hymns and carols were printed in a number of languages. For a week before the service, participants had practiced singing words to stanzas in Mandarin, Urdu, Hindi, Swahili, Spanish, Portuguese, Gaelic, and English.

The service of worship was outside in the dark. The nativity scene took place in an ancient cave hollowed out of a wall left from a centuries-old monastery. The worshipers stood.

The next morning at breakfast a young man from Burma said to an Englishwoman, "I have never spent Christmas so close to Bethlehem."

She answered with a chuckle, "And I've never been so far away from Harrogate."

Much of the learning about writing resources that include children in worship came after the service. What was made clearest to the writers by their own participation was keeping God as the focus of worship. What came as an insight to some as they wrote services of their own was the range of places they had at home where worship might include their neighbors.

Epiphany

The Sundays between Epiphany and Ash Wednesday are days to consider that all people are God's people. The work and words of Jesus' ministry are for all times and all places.

A church in the heart of a large metropolitan area had a mission festival called "People Serving People." The church has a reputation for serving those around it, many of them homeless and more of them hungry. But after this particular festival longtime members spoke with wonder at the work so few do for so many.

The festival began with the Sunday service of worship. A procession of all ages and human colors came down the center aisle with banners announcing their mission effort. There were twenty-two of them. Children played a Pachelbel canon on easy-to-play percussion instruments. The children's choir and a youth ensemble sang and supported the congregation in its singing. All teachers in the education program were recognized in a service of dedication.

After worship the banners were taken to the basement, where representatives sat at tables answering questions, showing pictures, and inviting parishioners' participation. School-age children and their parents gleaned information in order to complete a mission puzzle. They discovered that their church cooperated with other downtown churches to accomplish what no single one could do well—ministries among the homeless and chronically mentally ill. Churches all over the metropolitan area cooperated in food and clothing distribution. Churches and organizations cooperated in ministries to wandering and alienated teenagers, homeless families, newcomers to the country in need of English lessons, and children without a safe place to stay before and after school.

A father and his eleven-year-old son, intent on seeing everything, came to the conclusion that mission always involves cooperation. They were listening to two adults talking about overseas mission work of the denomination.

"Of course," one of them said, "much of the work is ecumenical."

"Wow, Dad!" the boy exclaimed. "That's the word we're looking for here," and he completed his puzzle. The puzzle helped children focus on the real intent of the festival. With so much to look at that is geared to the edification of adults, boys and girls can use their skills in research to ferret out fundamentals: The church is people serving people. There are no geographical limits to our mission.

The Road to Easter

Young children are at a disadvantage during Lent and Easter seasons. They are still learning of the events in the life, death, and resurrection of Jesus Christ. They do not yet have the ability to differentiate between "before I was born" and two thousand years ago. No matter the clever ways we find to explain time, they don't have chronological sense. It is for sound reasons that we do not teach history in first grade. As these boys and girls hear stories of Jesus, many grow to love him. They can sing "Hosanna" on Palm Sunday and become quite upset when they gather from TV specials that he has been killed at some time during the week.

Telling young children the whole story over and over again during Lent gives the edge they need to take part in church festivals that are steps along the road to Easter. Better that they see God's purpose in the journey rather than in isolated stops and starts along the way.

Older children are welcome storytellers and play givers, especially as Holy Week approaches. An adult advocate might spend the weeks in Lent with older children preparing stories to present to younger children the week before Palm Sunday. When the days come that the whole church shouts "Hosanna!" and "He is risen indeed!" the children should have heard the story enough times to be able to celebrate with other worshipers.

For several years a man who is active in community theater meets with eight- to ten-year-olds in his church to produce a combination of drama and readings. The young children see the production several times and become part of what he calls "mob scenes" as Jesus preaches, heals, and is praised at the triumphal entry to Jerusalem. The rest of the congregation witnesses the finished product on Palm Sunday during the education hour. Then everyone goes to worship.

"It reminds us all," the director says, "that when Jesus came to Jerusalem, it was not just for a parade. The children get us ready for the tough stuff that follows."

The production has not been the same each year, because the children use their own words in portions of the drama. The director believes that "by the time they get the story straight, they'll remember it, maybe all their lives."

He tells of how genuinely sad the whole cast of children was one year during a first reading of the death and burial.

"Then my little women came to the tomb and found it empty except for two boys 'in dazzling clothes,' one of whom said, 'Just kidding!'

"I handed him a copy of Luke 24:1–12 and said, 'Here. Read this and shape up. There are younger children learning from you.' "

Two of the children in the last production are in the minister's family. At lunch on Palm Sunday the four-year-old said, "Can we have Palm Sunday again next week? It's my favorite day."

"Harriet!" the eight-year-old shouted at her sister. "Next week is Easter! Don't you know anything?"

Harriet clapped her hands. "Hurray! Palm Sunday and Easter is my favorite day!"

"Mine too," her mother said.

Easter as a Season and the Day of Pentecost

There is festival enough in the service of worship on Easter Day so that very little need be done to accommodate children. If, in the order of service, the minister says, "The Lord is risen!" the children may be taught ahead of time to respond in loud voices, "He is risen indeed!" When it is repeated two more times the others in the congregation are likely to respond with appropriate enthusiasm.

In two or three sessions of church school and periods of education for worship, the boys and girls can learn to sing the congregational hymns for the service. Church school units at this time of year normally are about Holy Week events. In the weeks that follow, very often the sessions are about Pentecost and the early church.

The week before the Day of Pentecost the children might hear or read the story of God's Spirit coming during the Jewish feast of Pentecost. On the Day of Pentecost they are ready to praise God for the Spirit loosed among us in the church.

In a western mountain community the Day of Pentecost usually signals the opening of all passes and automotive traffic unknown for months. Three Protestant churches have a twenty-year tradition of worshiping together on that day. In making plans this past year, the new Episcopal rector questioned the other two pastors. "Why just three of our churches? Where are the Roman Catholics? Why not—"

"You're what we need, Geoff," the Presbyterian pastor interrupted. "John and I thought last year's service needed more fire and less wind. What shall we do?"

"First off," Geoff said, "let's invite all the churches around the four corners—the chapel and the churches in Marshall and around Wrightsville. Let's show ourselves and others that Christians can speak a common tongue."

"Say they come, where will they sit?" John asked. All the church buildings are small.

As they answered one another's questions the whole Day of Pentecost changed. They could worship at Four Corners Park, a small municipal park north of town where two state roads intersect. They could parade down Main Street with the children leading. How about a picnic? The three adjourned in order to check the interest of the other pastors.

The Presbyterian met with his regular Wednesday school class of third through sixth graders before calling any of his colleagues. He asked what the boys and girls thought of the Pentecost plans. They had only vague recollections of the combined service held each year. But a parade and a service in the park?

"Go for it!" a boy counseled his pastor.

"We could write letters to the kids in other churches," a girl suggested. "And maybe you could tell the *Independent* to print a news item," she told the minister.

"Are we going to have a band?" another child asked.

The minister was heartened by the children's clear interest in celebration. Some neighboring churches agreed to cooperate. The children talked at school with their friends, not inquiring about church affiliation, and together they believed they had a marching band.

"It may be slipping out of our hands," the Presbyterian minister said at a meeting of pastors.

"Just as it did in the second chapter of Acts!" The Episcopalian laughed.

The band grew as young people became interested. They

even had a director committed to the project. After Easter Sunday a delegation of pastors and laypeople planned the whole celebration. They would assemble at the Lutherans' parking lot and parade down Main Street with the band playing, children leading, and a county sheriff's car trailing. The service would be in the park and the picnic on the playground of Saint Mary's in the Mountains School.

Everything had gone together with harmony. "No one thought to ask," the rector said, recalling the whole experience, "what the band director was doing until it was almost at a point of crisis."

The Brethren pastor up the mountain called Geoff. "My son is in the band. He's been blowing 'Onward Christian Soldiers' on his trumpet for the last fifteen minutes. We're known, we Brethren, as a peace denomination. I must protest, Harding. I don't want him or anyone else 'marching as to war.'"

Before passing the protest to others on the committee, Geoff Harding went to his hymnal. If he could find other words to sing to that tune, he personally would teach the children, who in turn would teach the adults.

On the Day of Pentecost in the Lutherans' parking lot, the children assembled with Geoff as their leader. They practiced singing these words to the familiar tune:

> At the name of Jesus
> Every knee shall bow,
> Every tongue confess him
> King of glory now;
> 'Tis the Father's pleasure
> We should call him Lord,
> Who from the beginning
> Was the mighty Word.

> *Refrain:*
> At the name of Jesus
> Every knee shall bow,
> Every tongue confess him
> King of glory now.

The words were typed on an insert in the order of worship. The parading worshipers sang it over and over on their way to the park. After the service, people visited with one another and walked over to the picnic grounds.

The Brethren pastor shook Geoff's hand and gripped his shoulder. "Thank you with my whole heart. I have a new song to sing because of you."

Geoff replied, "My fourth-grade teacher taught me that hymn. She said if Christians had a national anthem, 'At the Name of Jesus' would be it."

The churches intend to continue cooperating each year on a Day of Pentecost parade, service of worship, and picnic. They are learning to understand one another's words and ways.

Other People's Festivals

When children invite their friends to their festivals at church they need help in knowing how to be hospitable. In order to teach other boys and girls what the occasion calls for in behavior, they need to know themselves.

A children's Easter festival to which each child was permitted to bring one guest turned out to be a party. One host was as surprised as his guest. The last festival he had been to with his father was "just one cartoon after another," and that is what he had prepared his friend for. They were five years old.

A seven-year-old who attends a Baptist church school tells often of his experiences at his grandparents' church, which is Greek Orthodox. He invited a classmate to spend Easter with him on an overnight expedition.

"George and his dad told me everything that would happen, and it all did," Jon told his class the next week. He dictated his class report to his mother so she could write it down.

We went to Indiana on a Saturday, and we got to stay up very late, past midnight. We went to church at night, and it was dark. Everybody got a candle and went outside. We went around and around the church. It was three times, I am sure. The priest was all dressed up like Jesus, but different. He knocked three knocks on the door and said something in Greek. Somebody yelled back at him from inside. He knocked three knocks again. And then when he knocked again, somebody opened the doors. All the lights were on. It was gorgeous. We all had the Lord's Supper, even babies. The priest gave us each some on our tongues. Before we went home we got Easter bread and a red Easter egg. George's grandfather tried to break our eggs and not his, and he did. So we ate them.

Jewish families are often eager to have a Christian family at their Seder service and meal at Passover. Although the story of the exodus is told and everything is explained, it helps children to know ahead of time what is going to happen. A child from the family may review the story or read a book with a guest about the exodus.

A child of nine whose mother comes from a United Church of Christ background and whose father is a Reform Jew regularly attends church and church school with her mother. When she was seven, Passover and Holy Week came at the same time. She remembers the time as a high point in her life.

"I took my U.C.C. cousin to Nana Stern's for Seder and my Jewish cousin to church and Easter dinner with my mother and father."

THE CHURCH FAMILY CELEBRATES

Milestones along the path of a congregation rightly are noted and celebrated by everyone. Many observances relate to the building in which the congregation worships—ground breaking, dedication, and anniversaries. Some celebrations are recognitions of members' accomplishments—

retirements, homecomings, and birthdays. Their appropriateness in the church depends on how such events relate to the worship of God and love of neighbor.

"A Century in This Place"

Although church members worked for a year, the hundredth anniversary of the first service of worship in the sanctuary began for the seated congregation with trumpets, French horn, trombones, and tympani.

The minister and the people said:

"Sing aloud to God our strength,
  shout for Joy to the God of Jacob.
  Blow the trumpet on our festal day."

By the time the two flags of the denomination and congregation, the credal banners, and the choir went by in procession, children throughout the congregation were staring in wonder. When a second grader walked briskly to the lectern with an open Bible, they knew it was their festival too.

A sixth grader visiting from another church was most impressed by a litany response:

"We pray for children and grandchildren who will worship in this place."

She told someone who greeted her after the service, "I came with my aunts to hear the music, but it's the prayer I remember. It makes me think of growing up and coming to church with my kids."

One of her aunts said, "I'll remember what the preacher said: 'One life is never long enough to finish God's work.' I'm counting on you and your kids, Amanda."

The younger children were out on the street after the service blowing bubbles as the church bell tolled one hundred times. Oldest members of the congregation were helped into horse-drawn buggies and chauffeured to the place where the celebration continued. Children, youth, and adults sang and rang bells. Two members showed their original sound and slide show. Oldest members were recognized and everyone ate.

Many people worked on arrangements for the day. A couple coordinated the efforts. The clergy advised throughout.

Dedication of an Old Building for a New Use

One Saturday at a small shopping center between a laundromat and a paint store, balloons and wind socks were whipped by the characteristic wind of the valley. Children were giving out vouchers for one hour to one full day of child care at this place. The banner above the door did not say "Grand Opening," but it did say OPEN HOUSE. On the two plate-glass windows where the sign used to say, ADULT BOOK STORE XXXX OPEN EVERY DAY 11 TO 11, people saw a purple cross and the words CHURCH OF THE MASTER AND CHILD-CARE CENTER OPEN EVERY DAY M–S 7–7, SUNDAY 12–6.

The pastor was the grandmother of the children who were outside dispensing vouchers. She said that ever since the bookstore opened she had prayed and planned to supplant it with a safe place for children and room enough to meet for worship. All visitors on Saturday were invited to the 2 P.M. dedication service on Sunday.

It was a service of worship in the middle of the room surrounded by shelves of toys and equipment, a rocky boat, little chairs and tables. There was a choir in front to lead the singing of hymns for a half hour. The minister greeted everyone, and then boys and girls conducted the service up to the time of the sermon. There was a time for people in the congregation to express their hopes for the new church and child-care center. After the minister preached there was an offering and benediction. People lingered to talk, drink spiced tea, and eat open-faced sandwiches.

Boys and girls were an integral part of the new church, with an understanding of their importance as contributing individuals. They exhibited a poise characteristic only of children who have been schooled in their responsibilities and counted on to come through for the community.

Homecoming at a Ninetieth Anniversary

A spin-off of a celebration in a well-attended Lutheran congregation in the upper Midwest was a party for three men from the congregation who had become ordained ministers. The observance of ninety years on the land had been held at the congregational service of worship that morning.

The party began in the side yard with grilled bratwurst, fresh tomatoes, and roasted corn on the cob. The boys and girls played without adult direction until time to eat. A man in the congregation invited the children to sit in a particular place. When everyone had eaten, he called the party goers to order.

"It isn't often we have three visiting ministers and all sons of the church. I've asked the children to sit up front here so that Alan, John, and Bill can talk to them. I expect the rest of you will want to listen too."

The three men were a director of family services, a bishop of the denomination, and a chaplain in the U.S. Navy. The layman asked them to tell the children what they remembered the clearest about growing up in Messiah Lutheran Church. The children were attentive.

Alan, the director of family services, said that growing up in their small town he got to know all kinds of people he wouldn't have known in a big city with neighborhoods. He had known the richest family in town and the poorest. He had walked to school with a boy whose uncle whipped him until he bled. The boy ran away, and when the police found him, he didn't have to live with his uncle anymore.

"I remember, more than anyone else, Pastor Hoffman — and my Sunday school teacher, Mrs. Evelyn Meyers. She wrote to me once a month when I went to Iowa for college and seminary."

John became a bishop. He remembered Pastor Hoffman too. He said the church was the center of the community in those days.

"It was the place to be when I was growing up. I sang in the choir, recited scripture, and played Joseph in the Christmas pageant. When I was in Luther League we were busy doing things all the time."

The teacher John remembered was a man who later won a seat as an assemblyman in the legislature and after that went to Washington, D.C., as a congressman.

Bill, the Navy chaplain, said his best teacher was Pastor Hoffman.

"I was a farm boy. I knew only the kids in my Sunday school class from here until I came into town to go to high school. I couldn't even come to confirmation class when everyone else did. It worried my folks that my older brother wasn't confirmed. But Pastor Hoffman came out to the farm one day to talk about Confirmation.

"He said, 'Now, boys, I'll have a class for you on Saturdays at eleven. That will give you time to walk in here and back home in the daylight.' "

Then Bill said, "When I told Pastor Hoffman I was going to seminary, he said, 'You're kind of shy, Bill, but God doesn't play tricks on us. If you heard the Lord calling, you go. Do you understand me?' I did and I went."

The master of ceremonies asked if the children had any questions.

"Where did you live?"

"Who lives there now?"

"Did you have to walk to school?"

"Did you play on a team in high school?"

The ministers enjoyed the question time and joked with the children in a way they found humorous as well. The congregation sang one stanza of "Jesus Shall Reign," and everyone went home from the party.

There are other occasions for homecoming parties in the

church, and telling stories of the people of God at work is an appropriate activity whenever they occur. Children gain insights into their work as Christian disciples as they meet admirable adults who, years before, read scripture and sang hymns of praise in the same place as they do now. The church at times like these is a first-rate vocational school.

Farewells

Saying good-bye to someone who seems indispensable and irreplaceable is a bittersweet experience in a congregation. Often it is a good time for the persons who are leaving, and the community is glad for them. At the same time, some who stay behind are grieving. Almost everyone is ambivalent.

When Mrs. Tran retired from her longtime job as director of child care in the church, it was to go to Chicago to live with her son's family. She was eager to do it, but she knew how much she would miss her work.

She had come to the United States from Vietnam with the first refugees and had acted as go-between, translator, and interpreter with the school system. On Sundays she brought an alert, scrubbed cluster of children to church school. As time went on she worked as a volunteer instructor in the baby and toddler nursery and then became director of the child-care program as well.

She was decisive and plain-spoken in her work but always exceedingly modest when praised. The people of the church who planned her farewell took this modesty into consideration. They told her there would be a tea to thank her on the second Sunday of June between church school and worship. They explained that the city newspaper wanted to photograph her with some children.

The tea was very informal. Mrs. Tran sat talking with parents and children, unconcerned with photographers.

The pastor called for silence, and as people stood around Mrs. Tran, he said, "We asked the children you have cared for over these years, " 'How shall we show our appreciation? What would she like?'

"One after another said, 'Let's give her flowers, lots of flowers.' "

At that point teenagers she had cared for came in single file, each handing her a peony. Behind them were boys and girls from the child-care center, each adding a peony to her bouquet. And finally, parents with babies in arms gave her even more peonies for an enormous bouquet.

Everyone was laughing.

"Thank you! Thank you!" Mrs. Tran exclaimed. "You know I love flowers. I do! I do!"

The next day there was a page of pictures in the newspaper of this simple thirty minutes of tea and peony exchange. Above the pictures was the caption: *Nazarene children show their thanks to Mrs. Tran with peonies and laughter.*

When a northern New England pastor was called to a southern New England church, the congregation knew he would have to go.

"They need him down there," a deacon said. "He and the family can come back and visit. We're best of friends."

The final farewell, for there were many at church and in town, was on the village green across from the church. It was a picnic supper to which anyone could bring anything and eat with everyone else. Children, young people, and adults played together and separately as they chose.

"You would think," a townswoman said to someone arriving after the picnic supper, "that we are glad they're going. We aren't at all; but you know the saying, 'The Lord giveth, and the Lord taketh away.' We're making the best of a bad thing."

At eight o'clock, the minister called out, "Thank you all for coming. It was a great picnic. Play as long as you want. I have to go to choir practice. It's my last opportunity to sing with this spectacular group."

He went into the church, only to discover that choir practice had turned into a talent show in his honor. There had been no auditions. Just as at the picnic, anyone could bring anything so that everyone might enjoy it. It was, of course, a great show.

There are many other occasions in the church year and the day-to-day life of a congregation that might stir a community to worship and celebrate. St. Andrew's, St. David's, St. George's, St. Patrick's, and St. Thomas's Days stir particular portions of the United Kingdom, Ireland, and India. Reformation and All Saints' Sundays rouse certain denominations in North America and parts of Europe.

There is, literally, no known end to the variety of local observances and celebrations among God's people. New occasions, new acquaintances, and new understandings of who we are and to whom we belong rouse us as a multitude keeping festival.

SUMMARY

Festivals in the church are memorable events celebrating special days in the church year and milestones in the life of the congregation.

With adult help, children can participate in the festivals as more than spectators.

With preparation, children can participate in festivals of other faiths.

All festivals of the church should be inclusive of children, persons with handicapping conditions, and the elderly.

5

Making a Difference

In congregations where work is part of a shared ministry with children, boys and girls learn early about "disciple work." What we do with people in need can make a difference in otherwise grim lives. Most disciple work calls for cooperation with adults and young people in the church. Some of it depends on the efforts of many congregations in the community, the country, or the world. It is significant work in the interests of others. We do it in obedience to God as we carry out the Great Commandment, loving our neighbor as ourselves. Working for and with the neighbor is the final step in bible study—action. The ministry of Jesus is full of words of action addressed to his disciples: Follow me, go, proclaim, stand up, listen, watch, come, give, pray, eat, drink, remember, teach, baptize.

We are all more likely to remember what we do in the process of learning than what we read or hear about. Children with adult role models around them who respond actively to others' needs are quick to act themselves.

A woman who manages a child-care facility tells of a four-year-old girl's reaction to the TV news.

"One evening after the other children had left, I brought Loni into the kitchen. She told me her mother was in Mexico 'helping people.' Her father was to come and get her from child care. I turned on my TV set on the counter, and the news was in progress. A woman was reporting about an earthquake, but I didn't pay attention as to where. Loni did.

" 'Mexico,' the child said, and her back stiffened. 'Mommy is there. Maybe Daddy and I will go there to help those people.'

"Just about then her father came and explained that Loni would be away for about two weeks.

" 'There's been an earthquake in Mexico,' he said. 'Our church is in charge of the relief operations in one location. My wife has already gone.'

" 'I thought you worked over at Jim's station,' I said to him.

" 'I do,' he answered. 'But you see, we're Adventist. We go wherever our neighbors need us. Human need comes first.' "

THE IMPORTANCE OF ROLE MODELS

Within the life of a congregation where children mingle with young people and adults, the choosing of role models is somewhat mysterious. Children do this all by themselves, no matter to what lengths we go to provide admirable, stable, adult companionship.

A seven-year-old girl and her nine-year-old brother were enrolled in a church-related school in the Middle East while their parents were engaged in famine relief on the horn of Africa. The boy adjusted quickly and related to both children and adults easily. His sister was reticent except with her brother. The faculty decided to appoint a young male teacher to be her grown-up friend. She accepted him but remained solitary, except with her brother.

One day the man said to her as they worked together on an art project, "I wish we knew what would make you smile and laugh, Suzanne."

"When Renny and I were in Bangladesh — " she began but stopped.

The teacher waited.

"Mr. James, there is nothing to do here!"

"We're doing something," he said, "and you're cracking good at it."

"But" — she grimaced — "it doesn't make any difference."

Then the story unfolded. When they were with their parents in home schooling, the two children worked alongside them on certain tasks. Now, only her brother remembered those days and talked with her about living like that again.

The faculty went back to work on Suzanne's "case," as they called it. Some high school students were deeply involved in volunteer work among the poor, but the school had only rarely involved children in community assistance. That could change, they agreed.

Suzanne and Mr. James remained good friends, but her role model became Christine, a seventeen-year-old high school girl. She chose Christine the first day the children in her class observed an art workshop at a small school for mentally retarded children. Without Christine and her school's involvement, the seven-year-old child could not do her disciple work. But when the parts of the body of Christ work together each is empowered to make a difference in the lives of neighbors.

We need not launch a full-blown program in which adults take on the cargo of children on their way to discipleship. But we do need to be intentional about including significant service to others as part of their biblical education in the church. In congregations where there is an expectation of the inclusion of children in work with the neighbor, a team of one adult and one or two children doing what none could do as well alone is an example to others within the congregation.

In a Roman Catholic parish in a deteriorating inner-city neighborhood, Father Gratz tells children as they prepare for their first Communion that adult worshipers will teach them one-on-one how to work for the good of others.

"I am a matchmaker," he says. "We have so much work in the parish! I don't beg any grown man or woman to help *me*. No! I stand before them with children at my side and say, 'Here's what we have to do.' Then we all go to work. O'Hara at the diocesan office says I'm role-modeling. I'm doing nothing of the sort. We're the poor doing Christ's work among the poor in this city."

Father Gratz learned how to do disciple work from Sister Mary Frances when he was a "street urchin" on Chicago's near North Side over forty years ago. He did not know his parents. He lived with his grandmother, whose prized possession was a small TV set with a magnifying device in front of it. She sent the child outside so that she could watch her programs "in peace." The boys on the street nicknamed him "Garbage." He found that sitting on the parochial school steps kept him out of trouble. He thinks he was about four when he met Sister and told her his name was Garbage.

"Nobody's name is Garbage," she said harshly. "What's your real name, son?"

"Jimmy, I s'pose," he told her.

"Then Jimmy you are. God makes no garbage of little boys with all that you have. Look at you. Two arms, two good legs, eyes, ears, mouth, and mind. We need you in this parish, Jimmy. There's work to do."

And off to work they went. Day after day they went to the market, to the sick and elderly, and to Spanish classes, where he learned the language by exposure to Sister's lessons.

One morning as he waited for her on the steps, the older boys were playing ball on the sidewalk. As Jimmy ran after the ball, one shouted at him, "Get outa here, Garbage. Quit messing up our game." Sister Mary Frances materialized at that moment, gathered the boys, and told them what she later told Jimmy again and again.

"There is no such thing as human garbage. I'll tell you what a lot of us are—we're leftovers, ready to be used for God's good purpose. When Jesus fed the crowd on the far side of the Sea of Galilee, there was enough food so that all were filled and twelve baskets of leftovers besides. Come on, boys. We're none of us better or worse than the other. We're Christ's leftovers waiting to be useful, all of us."

Father Gratz doesn't know what happened to those particular leftovers. But he knows he survived and then thrived in the city, working alongside Sister Mary Frances and then putting others to work somewhere else.

"I've made fun of O'Hara's role-model talk, but Sister is probably mine," he admits. "She was never long on gentleness, because she was busy giving us work to do. But she insisted on my understanding who I am and to whom I belong, all the while I was doing the work of Christ."

YOUNG CHILDREN MAKING A DIFFERENCE

Sons and daughters of men and women who take them along on their works of compassion grow up in a caring community. These adults are generally the first to enlarge their circle by inviting the children's friends to work with them. Preschool, kindergarten, and early elementary boys and girls need close supervision as they work in the interest of others. They have not tested their abilities, and their intuition is based on incomplete or erroneous conclusions about the world. (Spider-Man climbs walls; maybe I can.)

Young children, precisely because they do not know what is involved in an act of mercy, sometimes surprise us with their effectiveness. We should commend them at the same time that we continue to offer close supervision and more guided experience.

A boy of six on a Christmas shopping trip with his mother and aunt disappeared in a crowded suburban store.

"Let's go to the toy department before we panic," his

mother said. No sign of Alex. The women separated and searched, agreeing to meet in three minutes at Information in the mall. The child's aunt heard Alex's voice and followed it to where Santa Claus puts a child on his lap for a price and a photo opportunity.

Alex was explaining to a sales supervisor that "the man in the Santa Claus suit was unkind to this little girl." The "little" girl was four, and Alex was taking care of her until he could find her father. The children were not upset at the time. Alex had spoken out stalwartly for justice, and his companion trusted him.

On the way home in the car Alex told his story. The little girl had walked up to Santa Claus to talk to him. Alex heard him say, "The girl who takes the pictures ain't here just now. Go get your mother."

The little girl told the man what she wanted for Christmas, and he told her to go away.

"She cried," Alex said, so he talked to her. Her father was lost in the store, she told him.

"I was very angry at that Santa Claus," Alex went on. "I told him he should be nice to her, because she still 'believed.' He told me to shut my face. Then the man from the store came, and I told him what happened. Then Mindy came."

Alex's mother told him she was glad he had been kind to the little girl.

"I know you learned how to be a guide to lost children around church, but all of the grown-ups in the store might not know how to help one another as we do at church. Stick with us next time. OK, Alex?"

"That Santa Claus was disgusting," Alex complained. "If I could write a letter I would tell the president of that store to fire that Santa Claus."

"We don't know what Santa's boss is saying to him right now," Mindy said. "He may be in trouble. Or maybe you taught him something, Alex. Who knows?"

We need to encourage children's spontaneous attempts at compassionate action. They are evidence of their empathy for the helpless, weak, or unprotected. The last thing in the world we want to do in the face of their boldness is laugh at them. We should, of course, recall such times with them with pleasure but never derision.

Young children are serious in their intent and can perform a useful ministry just by being themselves in the company of an adult engaged in ministry.

A minister of a mission-supported parish to several rural churches tells of sitting at the kitchen table in a home with a three-year-old boy and his mother. The phone rang. A distraught woman was calling for the minister from a hospital in the nearest city. She had just received very sad news about her four-year-old daughter. The hospital personnel had given her the minister's number, and she had finally found her. When the minister hung up she told the woman and three-year-old Jesse why she had to leave.

Then she said, "I have some idea how to comfort adults at times like this, but what do you do with children?"

"I will go with you," Jesse said. "I will be four years old on December tenth."

The minister brightened. "What would you say to the sick girl, Jesse?"

"I would play with her."

"She's in bed," the minister reminded him.

"Mom played with me when I had the chicken pox."

It was agreed that Jesse would go to the hospital. On the way over in the car the two talked about hospitals and the care of sick children.

The minister and child walked into the building, waved at the workers at the reception desk, and went past a sign specifying where young children were permitted to go. The minister greeted familiar employees, who patted Jesse on the head without questioning his right to be there. In the child's room, the mother immediately took the minister's attention and Jesse played with Luann.

After a time the minister asked, "Would you like me to lead us all in prayer before Jesse and I go?"

"Oh, yes, please do," the sick child's mother answered.

When the minister finished, Jesse announced, "Now I will pray." And he did.

Jesse's mother was pleased to hear how he had acted. "It's awesome to know he did that at his age," she said. "He's such an ordinary kid."

The Bible is filled with examples of ordinary people doing extraordinary things. Peter caught fish for a living. Who knows what the men were like who brought their sick friend through the roof so that Jesus could heal him? Amos was a shepherd. Joseph was a carpenter. And the Jewish women in Old and New Testaments did not have the advantage of education.

OLDER CHILDREN MAKING A DIFFERENCE

Boys and girls nine to twelve years of age have a keen sense of justice. "It isn't fair" is condemnation, not a mere opinion. Many would like to change what they find wrong, but they don't know how. Because injustices around us require political action, the men and women in our congregations who understand power structures are best equipped to work with outraged older children.

In an urban township boys and girls ten and over were recruited by a nonpartisan organization to accompany disabled and elderly persons to the polls in a primary election. The project was well-organized, children were informed of procedures, picked up after school, and taken to their neighborhoods.

Two boys reporting on the activity the next Sunday in church school were indignant. They had both taken elderly persons to vote, only to find that the room was down two flights of stairs in a church.

"It took my woman an hour," one complained.

"An hour, Brad? An hour?" one of his classmates challenged.

"Well, a long time anyway. A man came by and helped her. I tried to help, but I didn't know what was right to do."

Their teacher was interested. He said, "I think that problem is something we can do something about. If you really care about those people who have trouble getting out to vote, we can speak up for them."

The teacher's idea was to mobilize the children to protest. The minister's idea was to organize a letter-writing campaign from children, youth, and adults assisting on Election Day. The president of the township board is an elder in their church. He suggested mobilizing, writing letters, and bringing an equal number of children and voters to a board meeting.

"I know," he told the boys and girls, "that my mother would come with you, and I think plenty of her friends would too. It's good to lose your patience when folks who should know better goof."

The two boys and their teacher talked to the woman who recruited the children. She and her daughter volunteered to start a telephone chain of all the names on their lists of voters and young assistants. Over a hundred letters went to the president of the town board. A "petition" came from the schoolchildren. Ten people, five of them children, asked and answered questions at a board meeting. A reporter from the weekly newspaper interviewed them afterward, and a photographer took pictures for the next issue. The story was under MUNICIPAL BUSINESS, not SCHOOL AFFAIRS. The headline was TOMORROW'S VOTERS CARE TODAY.

The minister told the congregation in a sermon that for a moment when two boys in the church took their consciences into the community, justice stamped out injustice and kindness killed thoughtlessness. On Election Day in November, only two polling places were inaccessible to wheelchairs and persons using walkers.

In the same densely populated township a knottier problem arose among persons with disabilities: The curbs were not ramped for electric wheelchairs, making the places of business inaccessible. The older children in the township, giddy with success from Election Day, wanted to be their advocates. They supposed they could form a telephone chain, write letters, and appear at a township board meeting and in the newspaper as they had before. No. This time the issue involved a great deal of money (or the lack of it), and that changed all the rules. The president of the township board told the children in fourth, fifth, and sixth grades to write to their elected state and national representatives. He said one letter from each class was OK, but each letter should be handwritten.

"When I get a letter written by anyone under eighteen I take it very seriously. I think they will too," he told them. He helped them say what they wanted to in very plain language. He suggested they ask children in other churches and in the synagogue to write letters as well. They did.

No one really knows how much good the letters did. Everyone involved knows they called attention to the problem. The Community Church in the heart of the commercial district called a pastor who rode down the highway in his wheelchair, because he could not use the sidewalks. No one arrested him, but motorists and bus drivers were very careful. Work began on standardizing ramped curbs with money from federal, state, and local sources.

It was a hard lesson for the children to learn: If justice is served it doesn't matter who gets the credit or fame. We work in obedience to the Great Commandment so that good comes from our efforts.

ACTS OF MERCY

Although older boys and girls need the counsel of more experienced persons in social ministry, there are acts of mercy they can carry out by themselves. Teachers, ministers, and church officers might learn of places children can be of help. Or the children themselves see the needs and respond. We teach love of neighbor in the church and should not be surprised at the serious responses of children.

Here are three examples of significant acts of mercy performed by nine- to twelve-year-olds. Sometimes they needed help, knew it, and asked for it. The recipients returned the kindnesses in unexpected ways. Remembering the needs of others became in each situation a way of life for a child of God whose vocation it is to love God and neighbor.

Bringing Comfort Where There Is Grief

In a small rural community with much poverty among families who own no land, the oldest child in a family of seven children ran away when he was sixteen. His twelve-year-old brother was furious.

"We need his money," he told the minister. "What my sister and I bring in is peanuts compared to what he made."

"If you and Weezey are good workers," the minister said, "the Grahams might hire you in the greenhouses."

"We'll work, all right," he promised.

The minister knew that there was addiction and abuse in the family, and that each child would find his or her own way out of the home. The children saw the church as their refuge. The mother and father ignored it as best they could.

The eight-year-old in the family grieved for her oldest brother. Her teacher at school told the minister the child had stopped functioning.

One afternoon as the minister met with the after-school group she asked, "How can we help Helen? She misses Ralph so much that she's stopped learning at school."

"My Mom won't let me play with her unless she comes to our house. I could ask — " a girl volunteered.

"No, Karen, that's not what's buggin' her," a boy interrupted. "She doesn't want to play that much. She wants to work like her older brothers and sisters. They all work because their mother and father don't. See, Ralph had just bought his bicycle and was going to teach her to ride. Then she figured she'd deliver things to people and get money."

"Good!" the minister said. "Can anyone teach her to ride a bicycle? Who's got a bicycle?"

There weren't many, and there were fewer offers to give lessons. The meeting adjourned. The minister says she believes in leaving things unresolved when younger minds than hers might go to work. The same group met on Saturday to help unload and sort clothes and household goods from suburban churches near New York City.

The driver of the van was enchanted by the young helpers. "They're right out of Charles Dickens!" he said. They gave the driver cocoa before he turned around to drive home. They thanked him for all he brought.

"You don't have an extra bicycle somewhere, do you?" one of them asked. They told him about Helen and Ralph and Weezey and the others.

"I'll tell you what we ought to do," he said to the group. "You teach Helen to ride. Tell me when she knows how. Then I'll look for a bicycle someone is no longer using."

Karen taught Helen to ride. It didn't take long, because Helen was fearless in her determination. They took turns riding after Helen knew how. In a few weeks, when the two came to the after-school meeting, the minister announced the arrival of another load from the south.

Helen said, "I'll be here to help. I'm the only big kid in my family who doesn't work."

That Saturday Helen got her bicycle. At first she was speechless. Then she bit her bottom lip and cried. "Finally, I can go to work," she announced.

The man who drove the van wanted to hear the details. He drank cocoa and asked questions.

"Who taught her to ride?" he asked.

"Karen did," several answered.

"No," Karen insisted. "All I did was let her use my bike. I don't know how to teach anybody anything. I'm only nine years old."

The van driver smiled. "Karen, you're a Christian. So am I. We share what we have, and good things come to those around us." Then he turned to Helen. "Karen taught you to ride on her bicycle. Don't forget to teach someone else on yours."

Helpless Except for the Help of Others

Ed Pinckney was a thirty-two-year-old, six-foot-four-inch 196-pound coach when he lost the use of his legs in an automobile accident. For therapy he swam; for stimulation he competed all the way to English Channel swimming; for enjoyment he taught inner-city children to swim. The last activity began when a city pool closed on Memorial Day after a gang-related fight. Ed's pastor in a very large Baptist church in the neighborhood of the pool asked him to estimate what it would cost to reconstruct the indoor pool that had been built in the church in 1923.

On the same day in the same church a retired city employee who at one time had advised the mayor gathered with an after-school group of girls to teach them good nutrition. No one was interested. The topic was "No Swimming Pool This Summer."

"We'll have to protest to the mayor," the woman told the girls. "But you need the support of hundreds of children."

"Oh, Ms. Hawkins! You don't mean it! We don't know hundreds of children," an eleven-year-old whined.

"I think I can teach you what to do," she told them. And the girls set to work.

More than a week later Tyrone Reese, ten-year-old mascot and protector of Ed, told him he thought the city pool would open after all. In fact, he said, someone from City Hall was coming to speak at Bethel Church that very afternoon.

"I'll take you over," Tyrone volunteered.

Ed found out on the way to his church that Tyrone had signed a paper in support of the pool, and the number next to his name was 309.

"What did you agree to do when you signed that paper?" Ed was suspicious. After all, he was working with his pastor on specs for a pool in that very church.

"We, the undersigned," Tyrone sang out, "promised to come to this meeting and bring one more person."

"And you're bringing me, is that it?" Ed asked.

"That's it," Tyrone agreed.

There were close to five hundred children and young people in the sanctuary. There were three representatives from City Hall and four boys and girls from sixth, seventh, and eighth grades to ask them questions. Ms. Hawkins called the crowd to order.

The unwavering line from City Hall was, "No supervision, no pool." The crowd was murmuring.

Ed whispered to Tyrone, "Let's go up front." Tyrone guided Ed's chair, even though he was quite capable of managing it himself.

Ms. Hawkins stood and introduced Ed without a notion of what he was about to do.

"I can supervise a pool," he declared, loudly enough not to need a microphone. "And Tyrone, here, can see that I get there."

The crowd cheered.

The city employees were not ready for so sudden a change in atmospheric conditions.

Ms. Hawkins spoke. "We're close to an agreement here, boys and girls. We'll let you know the outcome. Thank you for your support. Good-bye."

Ed supervised the pool. He taught young children to swim. Older children learned endurance in the water from young persons who already knew the basics. One after another, swimmers qualified for lifesaving.

When the pool closed on Labor Day there were cameras and interviewers from a TV station.

"I didn't start anything," Ed Pinckney told the woman who interviewed him. "This rejuvenating of the neighborhood began with Ms. Hawkins and her class of girls at Bethel Church. Tyrone Reese brought me into the picture."

Plans for the indoor pool at Bethel Church are canceled. The existing pool serves a larger neighborhood, and the supervisor is there to be sure that neighbors serve neighbors.

Volunteering to Be a Friend

Ellen Chase, at eighty-five, told her pastor that she'd as soon walk the mile to church as wait for a ride. "But," she said, "I'd feel safer if someone younger would agree to walk along with me."

"I suppose 'younger' meant sixty-five," the pastor says, "but we found the perfect match in Julie Harbison, a nine-year-old, who always came to church and church school and volunteered."

Several weeks after the Sunday morning pattern was established, Ms. Chase asked Julie to be her guest at a restaurant the following Sunday. The child was delighted.

A buffet brunch was served. The child went back three times for hot food. She ate no bread and no ice cream.

"We never have hot food," she told Ms. Chase. "This is really good."

"Does your mother sleep in on Sundays?" Ms. Chase asked.

"Sometimes," Julie answered.

Ms. Chase spoke to the pastor. "That child was starved," she said. "I'll take her out every week, but we should find out what isn't working in that household."

Nothing much was working there, the pastor discovered. Julie's mother was an alcoholic with many physical ailments. Her husband had moved out with Julie's older brother. The father sent support money, but Julie had not seen him for months. She and her mother were eating what Julie bought at the market.

When Julie's mother was taken to the hospital, Ms. Chase asked Julie to stay with her for a while.

"You're a good companion," she told the girl. Ms. Chase had domestic help who taught Julie many things, the best of all being how to make hot food.

"It was not a permanent solution," the minister says, "but it is the church at our best at work in the hard lives of those who suffer without a whimper."

In a sermon he summed up the whole church's efforts in the interests of the neighbor.

"We are all jugglers for Christ, balancing acts of mercy and our possessions, hand to hand, child of God to child of God, all over the world, making a difference that needs to be made."

SUMMARY

The work children do that makes a difference in the lives of others is done in response to the Great Commandment in obedience to God and in loving relationship to the neighbor.

Children choose role models to emulate. The church can offer opportunities for children to do disciple work alongside admired persons engaged in an essential ministry.

Sometimes the church offers children their only opportunity to learn how to work in the interests of others with someone willing to teach.

The church encourages children to act as advocates for the weak and should not be surprised when they do.

The church needs to support and struggle with children on thorny issues that affect their lives in the community.

6

Long-Range Planning

The earth is the LORD's and all that is in it,
the world, and those who live in it.
—Psalm 24:1

Long-range planning is a matter of stewardship—living now as God's people who own nothing but are called to care for God's world and those who live in it. We are a people with a memory and a mission. We have always, since God created time, begun things in one age to be continued in another. What are we doing now?

Wise use of the land and what is over and under it does not threaten the lives and livelihood of living things. Peace and justice do not bring wars for our children to settle or die trying. Worship of God our Creator does not give rise to idolatry. Sharing food and worldly goods does not increase the number of hungry, ill-clad, and homeless persons in our midst. What is it we have begun? What in God's world is our mission?

What must we do? We ask the same question our forebears asked at Pentecost. The answer is the same. Repent. Turn around and start working for the One who was, is, and ever shall be God. The One who brought us out of bondage to worship God in the wilderness, the One who in Jesus Christ showed us what was worth living and dying for, the One who sends the Holy Spirit to live with us and beyond us with our children and our children's children: That's who.

And once we repent, what is it we do? Jesus told the rich young Jewish professional men of his day, and he tells us: "You have heard this from your youth. Love God and your neighbor." Worship God and work in the interests of others.

The people of God who gather around the long-range planning table are models whether they want to be or not. Others imitate them without realizing it. Few in the rising generation are so discriminating as an eight-year-old boy who spends an inordinate amount of time practicing on his violin but precious little on homework.

In exasperation his father told him, "We don't expect you to be President of the United States, but we want you to be able to read a ballot."

"Who would want to be President?" the child said. "All I want is to be like Yehudi Menuhin. He looks for kids like me who would rather play music than soccer and invites them to one of his schools. You have to know how to read to be a musician, Dad."

Halfway around the world from the Presbyterian musician who finds a model in a Jewish violinist, conductor, and philanthropist are Arab children at play in the Gebalia refugee camp in the Gaza Strip. They have two teams, "Jews" and "Arabs," in a game of tag. The "Jews" carry sticks and chase the "Arabs." When an "Arab" is tagged he or she must face a wall while the "Jew" may hit the child once with a stick. The object of the game, of course, is for "Arabs" to stay as far away from "Jews" as possible. Who at the long-range planning table are these children imitating? Do the rabbis, imams, prime ministers, presidents, and kings want the children to grow up to be like them?

In a city of 30,000 in the United States two children, ages seven and nine, found a tackle box in a defunct playground at the edge of the city center. In it were simulated drugs of sugar and grass clippings and colored slips of paper with transactions recorded on them. The children turned the box over to the police, who uncovered a make-believe drug ring whose members sold their packaged goods to other children. The police believed all entrepreneurs to be twelve years old and younger. They were not sure if the children were emulating their parents or being trained for the drug business. A city council member remembered children playing fireman or policeman in the playgrounds, not drug dealer. Are there men and women of God at the long-range planning table who can intervene, befriend, and serve as mentors to children who would rather play drug dealer than soccer or music?

There are hard-working clergy and lay persons who do not want to sit at that table.

"What's the use?" a woman said after working for years in a rural slum with older children who needed serious remedial education in order to perform at grade level. "My kids are alcoholics, abusers, and unemployed today, if they aren't in jail or dead. Well, not all of them, but most."

The woman and her co-workers had been both competent and compassionate. A church official at a public recognition of their accomplishments said, "Working here is no way to get rich. That is why we appreciate the richness you have brought in you and left in this place."

One of the "survivors," now a teacher in a church-supported boarding high school, says of his days in the country, "Those teachers brought us tickets to the future. There was a price — you had to do your work and tutor those kids who needed to know what you had just learned. And do you know what happened when I caught on to that? I developed what our high school counselors call 'self-esteem.' It wasn't true with me that I had to learn to love myself before I could love my neighbor. My teachers never gave up on me, and I never gave up on anyone I tutored. But I loved a whole lot of funny neighbors before I realized that I was OK too. I was shaving before I liked myself! I remember looking in the mirror one day and smiling back."

About the classmates who didn't work for the same tickets to the future, he said, "One step forward, two steps back is no way to get anywhere. It wasn't so much they didn't believe in themselves; I didn't think I would ever learn how to read out loud. They didn't believe they belonged to anybody. I knew I was a child of God. Those teachers knew who sent them there to work. They couldn't have endured without God."

And does the man teach the way he was taught?

"Probably not," he says. "These are different days, and the kids I teach are older. I tell them the 'Thou shalt nots' about having babies and taking drugs. I say, 'I want to see you here next year' or 'What do you want to be five years from now? Shut your eyes and dream. What do you see yourself doing?'

"One boy said to me, 'What do you see yourself doing, Mr. Martinez?'

"I said, 'Come back in five years, Evan. I'll be here.'"

GOD'S PURPOSE

Our long-range planning goes into effect no later than now. Whether witting or unwitting role models, we affect the future every moment after a child is born. The world of a newborn abandoned in a shelter by a drug-addicted mother is more incomprehensible and vast than the world seen by the first astronauts who walked in space. They were connected to their neighbors in their vehicles and at Ground Central. They had some grasp of the limitlessness they beheld and a mission of sorts to accomplish. The abandoned infant is an alien with no memory of home.

Our work as the people of God is to make homes for the displaced, misplaced, and disenfranchised. When Jesus preached in his home congregation, he read from the prophet Isaiah:

> The Spirit of the Lord is upon me
>   because he has anointed me

to bring good news to the poor.
He has sent me to proclaim
release to the captives
and recovery of sight to the blind,
to let the oppressed go free,
to proclaim the year of the Lord's favor.
—Luke 4:18–19

Then he rolled up the scroll and sat down. "Today," he said, "this scripture has been fulfilled in your hearing."

CARING AS A VOCATION

Stewards of humankind bring home to the homeless, company to the lost and lonely, and help to the helpless. Caring is the calling of the people of God, our vocation no matter what our occupation. Bringing the vocation of caring into the twenty-first century calls for role models now.

The eleven-year-old girl from Milwaukee who saw a twenty-one-year-old woman from Allentown, Pennsylvania, washing the feet and cutting the toenails of a barefoot man on Eighth Avenue in New York City has a role model. She and her father watched, neither saying a word. The young woman gave full attention to her job.

When she was finished, she picked up her basin and tools, stood up, and said to the man, "There you go, sir. Those feet are made for walking."

"Ma'am," the man replied, "I am grateful. You put me in mind of Jesus as you knelt down there."

"Is it all right to talk to her, Daddy?" the child asked.

"I think so," he answered.

She ran up to the woman and asked, "Where do you go to college to learn how to fix feet?"

The two visited for a few minutes, sharing bits of their lives with each other, and went their separate ways.

In A.D. 2020 there may be someone with sore feet near someone who went to college to learn to fix them. The admirable act and the style in which it was performed both lent themselves to emulation. "I want to do that," and "I want to be like her," are very close in meaning to an older child.

A younger child might act out in play the work of someone he or she admires. If we are serious about bringing up children to work in the interests of others, we need to be intentional about exposing them to compassionate caregivers and become conscientious about watching their play.

A five-year-old boy at child care played barber one afternoon, giving tips on winning horses at the tracks as he performed his duties.

At almost the same time another child passed aluminum potpie tins to each leader. "I cooked up a mess of it," she said, "because I knew you'd be too tired to fuss."

"Thank you very much, Cherie," a teacher said. "Who taught you to make such delicious food?"

"I'm just pretending, Ms. Black," the child replied. "Mama says every night, 'My fairy godmother is late again with supper. I guess I'll have to fix us something to eat."

The more children are made to feel at home in the makeshift shelters the church provides, the more direct and honest they will be in their play, and the more intentional we can be in teaching them to be merciful.

A man and woman, now grandparents, raised their children without prodding them into one career or another and remain somewhat surprised at the lifework and avocations they chose: nursing in a prison, caring for foster children, working with elderly Alzheimer's and dementia patients, directing a head injury clinic, teaching retarded adults — the list goes on.

Looking back, they recall applauding the children's weekend work at an old established residence for severely retarded persons. The parents remember working at church, tutoring children at school, helping with health care at a nursing home — and that list goes on too.

When a grandson chose his summer school courses they were home economics and babysitting. There was a woman living on his street who would teach him how to work with a young child who has motor difficulties. He thought those two courses would make him more qualified to do it.

"It's bred in the bone," one of his uncles commented. "We're all like that."

Becoming a merciful person and a useful neighbor is not genetic. It is a gift of the Spirit, the same Spirit that came upon Jesus. In God's world the stewards of humankind are called to a vocation of caring. They learn how best to care and how to teach others to care. Shared ministry escapes the boundaries of congregation, community, and generation. Role-modeling is an investment in work the model may not be around to see.

A CONFESSING PEOPLE

The summer Jill Huntly was ten years old and her mother was forty they went to Scotland to find their roots. In a Grampian church they found a portrait of Jill's great-great-grandfather, who had been pastor there. When they talked to the minister he invited them to come back the next day for Homecoming Sunday.

It was a new experience for both Jill and her mother, and when they got back to their own church they wanted Homecoming Sunday there.

The church schoolchildren thought it was a good idea. The young people thought it would be fun to have reunions with people who had moved away. The minister brought the matter up at the annual calendar meeting in September. There was opposition.

"We can't do that, Harry," a middle-aged man said. "There was too much bad feeling when some folks left."

"Let sleeping dogs lie," another man agreed. "Those were bad days, and we lost a lot of members."

The young people at the meeting were disappointed. An elder spoke in their support.

"We have members of all ages," he said, "who don't know what church fight you're talking about. We have had members move away who don't know what trouble you refer to. Give the kids a chance. Let's see who comes."

The minister was taken with the idea, but he remained silent during the discussion. The elders met and decided, as one woman said before she voted, "to give goodwill a whirl."

The steering committee promoted Westminster's Homecoming Sunday in the city newspapers, the synod newsletter, and an independent church-related periodical. There were letters to former members and clergy, where addresses were known. Homecoming Sunday was in March, near the anniversary of the founding of the church.

Young people and schoolchildren worked in pairs as hosts and hostesses at the celebration. All children were invited to submit entries in the art display of church life. Two children's choirs sang in the Sunday morning service. The minister explained to the swelled congregation that without the eagerness of the children and young people, the day would not have been set aside for homecoming.

After a planned-menu potluck dinner contributed by members for their many guests, a small cast gave a historical dramatization. A couple showed old slides, rapidly with no narration, and 8-millimeter films from the 1940s that made everybody laugh.

The minister rose afterward to pray and to pronounce the benediction. At the same time the elder who had expressed initial opposition to the idea of homecoming came forward and asked for attention.

He told everyone he was sorry he had opposed the celebration. "I was afraid," he said. "I didn't want old enemies to meet. I didn't know there would be no enemies here."

An elderly man stood up and spoke. "Don't be too sure,

Al," he growled. Then he laughed heartily. "For you who don't know me, I was the pastor who could not face controversy and could not sit down with enemies. I am pleased to be back at Westminster and grateful to witness the involvement of children and young people in church policy. We need you, we old folks do. And so do the people of God who will worship here when you are gone.

"Now I'll pray, Harry, if you don't mind," he said to the minister, "and you can say what you want afterward."

His was a prayer of confession from the "timid and fearful who hurt and kill people, ideas, and possibilities." He had written it in his date book, and he read it.

Then the minister of the congregation stood again. Everyone was at attention.

"Hear the good news!" he announced. "In Jesus Christ we are forgiven. Go in peace."

Let the people say Amen.

SUMMARY

Long-range planners need to consider ways in which children can associate with and learn from persons in order to become faithful, compassionate leaders in the twenty-first century.

The church can make a difference in the lives of children now who suffer deprivation and abuse by offering a haven in which to find friendship and work of worth to their neighbors.

Our work as a people of God is to make a home for the displaced, misplaced, and disenfranchised. Children can work along with adults and young people in these ministries.